Charity, Law and Social Justice

Francis Gladstone

CL

BEDFORD SQUARE PRESS | NCVO

Published by the
BEDFORD SQUARE PRESS of the
National Council for Voluntary Organisations
26 Bedford Square, London WC1B 3HU

© NCVO 1982

ISBN 0 7199 1084 6

First published 1982

Photoset by Method Limited
Woodford Green, Essex
Printed and bound in England by H. Ling Ltd
The Dorset Press, Dorchester, Dorset

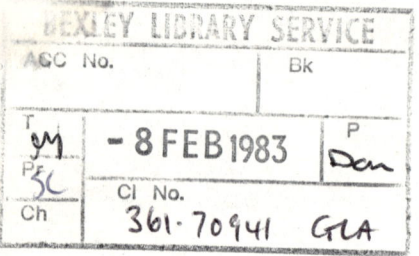

Contents

Acknowledgements

Many people have helped with the preparation of this study. I am particularly grateful to Christopher Zealley, Terry Lacey and Nicholas Hinton who encouraged me to begin it in the first place; to Adrian Longley and other lawyers who have borne with a layman's naive questions; to Dominique Dubois, Warren Kenton and Alison Roberts who have illuminated certain essential points; and to all the charities, and voluntary organisations which cannot at present be charities, who have shared with us their experiences of charity law.

The Chief Charity Commissioner, Dennis Peach, is an old friend and former colleague; his helpfulness and that of his fellow Commissioners and their staff is much appreciated. I am grateful, too, for the advice given me by staff at the Charities Division of the Inland Revenue.

But my greatest debts are to Gerry Smolka, who carried out most of the preliminary research and interviews and organised two fruitful conferences; to Judy Beer, who cheerfully bore most of the brunt of typing my indecipherable manuscripts; and to the staff of the Bedford Square Press who have published this book more quickly than it is fair to ask any publisher to work.

Finally, I am grateful to the City Parochial and the Wates Foundations, which helped to establish NCVO Policy Planning and which continue to support its work.

August 1982   Francis Gladstone

Introduction: A Reasoned Memorandum

*No organisation can be a charity and . . . include among its purposes
. . . bringing influence to bear directly or indirectly on Parliament to
change the general law of the land. . . . Thus it is very unlikely that it
will lie within any charity's purposes and powers to sponsor action
groups or bring pressure to bear on the government. . . . In the past it
was recognised that such activity lay well outside the true field of
charity although . . . there are other more traditional approaches
that have long been accepted as perfectly proper. . . . It is probably
unobjectionable for a charity to present a reasoned memorandum
advocating changes in the law.*

(Report of the Charity Commissioners, 1969)

This study is being published as a contribution to the continuing
debate on the law of charity. Various proposals for charity law
reform have been put forward in recent years but by no means
everyone accepts that any action is required. Members of the
present government are among the sceptics: according to the
Hon. Timothy Raison, the Home Office Minister responsible,
'Both the basic principles and the way in which they are
administered remain broadly satisfactory'; and in June 1981 the
Prime Minister told the Commons, 'We have no plans to bring in
legislation at the present time'.

It may be that the existing system is indeed 'broadly
satisfactory' but some practical difficulties persist and an
illustration may be useful. Although the law does not prohibit
political activity, charities do face some restrictions. Over the
years the Charity Commissioners have tried to assist charities by
providing guidelines on what they see as permissible. They have
never claimed, however, to know exactly where the boundaries
lie: 'We would emphasise that the law is based on a limited
number of decided cases and there is some danger in trying to
stretch them to cover the whole of the ground'.[1] Nevertheless, in
their view, 'The emphasis must be on rational persuasion'[2]: to
present 'reasoned memoranda' is acceptable, but not to organise a
march down Whitehall.

Not every charity, by any means, would feel hampered by such restrictions; and, as discussed later, not every lawyer would accept the Charity Commissioners' opinion that such restrictions exist. But that is little consolation to the small community association in the North of England refused charitable status on the grounds that it had campaigned for a pedestrian crossing. Theoretically it could appeal to the High Court but that is not as easy as it might seem: the cost of Amnesty International's recent appeal was in the region of £25,000 and this is not untypical.

THE REFORMISTS

It is widely accepted, in fact, that the difficulty of mounting an appeal to the High Court is unfortunate. Indeed, few would dispute that the existing system has a number of shortcomings; and there are some who believe that radical reforms are needed.

The last major overhaul of charity law was the Charities Act, 1960, which was based on the Nathan Committee Report,[3] presented to Parliament in 1952. By the early 1970s, however, increasing disquiet over the effects of charity law gave rise to a number of separate initiatives. Each of these started from different concerns but all identified problems which they felt warranted reforms.

First in the field was the Charity Law Reform Committee. This independent grouping was set up by a number of individuals and organisations, spurred by a decision, in 1971, to remove charitable status from the Humanist Trust. In February 1974, the Committee issued a pamphlet entitled *Charity Law – Only A New Start Will Do*[4] which began:

> *Which of the following organisations are Charities?*
> United Nations Association
> Disablement Income Group
> Amnesty
> Campaign against Racial Discrimination . . .
> National Council for Civil Liberties
> *None of them*
>
> *And which of the following are charities?*
> Eton College
> British Goat Society
> Vegan Society
> Voice of Methodism (against union with the Church of England)
> British Society of Dowsers
> *All of them*

After examining a number of difficulties encountered by charities and would-be charities, the pamphlet went on to propose a completely new category of organisations, Non-Profit-Distributing Organisations (NPDOs):

> The idea is very simple. NPDOs would be entitled to all the advantages of charities but without the attendant restrictions on their activities.... Among the types of body to benefit from the reform we would expect professional organisations, political parties and law reform organisations to be prominent.

The following year a sub-committee of the House of Commons Expenditure Committee turned its attention to charity law. Its report,[5] while stopping short of the completely new start advocated by the Charity Law Reform Committee, found all-party support for fresh legislation to achieve substantial changes including the removal of charitable status from most public schools.

In 1976 came the report of the Goodman Committee,[6] an independent inquiry set up in 1974 by the National Council of Social Service under the chairmanship of Lord Goodman. More systematic than those which had immediately preceded it, its proposals were rather more cautious although there was considerable common ground; and even the Goodman Committee, despite its caution, favoured new legislation.

Rumour has it that by 1979 a White Paper had been prepared, setting out legislative proposals but, if so, it was a casualty of that year's general election. The incoming government, despite its general advocacy of 'voluntarism', soon announced its view: the existing law was broadly satisfactory.

CHARITY LAW AND PUBLIC SCHOOLS

In one respect, at least, this view remains strongly disputed. Not everyone, it seems, finds it easy to see why public schools such as Eton, Harrow or Winchester should enjoy the benefits of charitable status. Indeed, not everyone accepts that such schools should be allowed to exist at all, at least in their present form.

In 1965, not long after the Labour Party's return to power after thirteen years in the wilderness, the Secretary of State for Education, Anthony Crosland, appointed the Public Schools

Commission 'to advise on the best way of integrating the public schools with the State system of education'. The government trod with care – it was not open to the Commission to recommend the abolition of public schools.

The practical obstacles to integration proved insurmountable and the Commission's compromise strategy,[7] an 'assisted places' scheme, did not find favour with the Labour Government* but some of its subsidiary proposals met with greater enthusiasm. Among these was the recommendation that

> Action should be taken to terminate the fiscal and similar reliefs of schools which are charities but which do not serve a truly charitable purpose.

When the Labour Party returned to power in 1974, its manifesto contained a commitment to remove charitable status from public schools but this was never implemented. More recently the Labour Party, reiterating its opposition to public schools, promised, among other steps, to remove their charitable status within a year of taking office.[8]

None of the other major political parties appears to favour a major onslaught on the public schools. But both the Liberals and the Social Democrats seem likely to favour action on their charitable status.[9] In particular, it seems that a large majority of SDP members would support the removal of the tax concessions enjoyed by public schools as charities. Clearly this aspect of charity law will remain politically controversial.

A NEW INITIATIVE

Against this background, the National Council for Voluntary Organisations (NCVO) recently decided that a new initiative was needed. To this end, a Charity Law Working Group was established to examine what changes in the law of charity and its administration might be useful and to work towards such changes. To assist the Working Group with this task, NCVO Policy Planning was asked to review the extensive literature on charity law and to engage in fresh consultations with voluntary organisations and other interested parties with a view to

---

*Its adoption twelve years later, in a modified form, by the present government, is somewhat ironic.

identifying and assessing the full range of policy options. The present study attempts to summarise the outcome of this work. It draws heavily on what others have written on the subject and also on over 100 interviews with representatives of voluntary organisations and other relevant bodies, conducted in the early months of 1982. In addition, during May 1982, NCVO held two consultative conferences, one on 'Political Activity and Charity Law' and the other on 'Charitable Purposes: Is The Law Too Narrow?', which were attended by representatives of over seventy voluntary organisations.

CHARITY, JURISPRUDENCE AND THEOLOGY

Charity law is essentially a branch of equity, that part of English law originally administered by the Court of Chancery. The origins of equity go back to the fourteenth century. As a result, charity law is founded less upon statute than upon the principles evolved over the centuries by the Court of Chancery as embodied in case law. Put another way, the rules and restrictions governing charities are judge-made law and no one should be surprised if the result of 600 years of judicial creativity is not the tidiest of laws. Even the most distinguished of judges have often admitted this. On one occasion, for example, a Master of the Rolls, Lord Sterndale, was driven to exclaim:

> The whole subject is in an artificial atmosphere altogether
> . . . and when one takes gifts which have been held to be
> charitable, and compares them with gifts which have been
> held not to be charitable, it is very difficult to see what the
> principle is on which the distinction rests.[10]

That is not to say there was originally no principle. Over the centuries, the word 'charity' has acquired separate legal and everyday meanings, neither of which corresponds exactly to the original, theological term. But theological principles had a profound effect on the early development of the concept of charity: the Court of Chancery was always headed by the Lord Chancellor and these 'keepers of the king's conscience', as they were known, were always ecclesiastics until 1529; it was not until 1672 that the practice of appointing clergy as Chancellors altogether ceased.

Hardly anyone today would claim that Britain is a Christian

society[11] despite its Established Church. That is not, of course, to say that Britain is an atheist society – nearly three out of every four adults (73 per cent) appear to retain some sort of belief in God[12] – but church attendance has fallen greatly since the time of our grandparents and only a minority see the church as giving adequate answers to the problems of family life, man's spiritual needs or the problems of our society.[13]

In a society where less than a sixth of the adult population are regular church-goers[14] it is not very surprising that 'charity', in everyday use, has come to be equated with alms-giving, nor even that some learned judges find it difficult to discern any principle in charity law. Given all this, it has seemed useful to trace back the concept of charity to its historical origins, not least because to do so casts a curious light on recent developments in the law. In particular, it is difficult to detect those clear distinctions the law now makes, not only between charity and poverty but also between charity and political activity. If, in doing this, the study concentrates on the Judaeo-Christian tradition, that is because it is there that the British concept of charity has its roots. It should be pointed out, however, that most of the major religions advocate not dissimilar principles.

KEY ISSUES

Part I of this study examines the evolution of the concept of charity from the earliest times up to today. But the modern law of charity owes as much to lawyers as to theologians, and the issues it raises have to be considered on their own merits. Part II, therefore, examines four key issues.

First, *public benefit*. Over the centuries Chancery lawyers have evolved the doctrine that 'public benefit' is the chief criterion of charity, in its legal sense. But, as said earlier, not everyone feels able to accept that the existence of public schools provides any broad public benefit; nor, for that matter, the existence of private medicine and various other expensive or exclusive institutions.

Second, *changing needs*. Lord Hailsham, the current 'keeper of the Queen's conscience', was undoubtedly right when he recently said, 'The legal conception of charity is not static, but moving and changing': the law of charity has always adapted to changing circumstances. But the twentieth century has brought unprece-dented economic and social change and there are those who feel that charity law, while 'moving and changing' is not moving and changing fast enough to keep up with changing needs.

Then there is *political activity*. 'A trust for the attainment of political objects has always been held invalid', ruled Lord Parker, in a leading case on charities and political activity.[15] Historically this is questionable: no judge had ever imposed such a sweeping ban before this case. As the law now stands, a considerable number of voluntary organisations see the case-law restrictions on political activity (and the Charity Commissioner's extrapolation of them) as an unwarranted muzzling of charities' freedom of expression.

Lastly, there is *regulation*. Three bodies supervise the benefits and restrictions of charitable status – the courts, the Charity Commissioners and the Inland Revenue. Some see the result as nothing short of disastrous: organisations which genuinely benefit the public suffering restrictions or being denied charitable status altogether while a substantial number of so-called charities are nothing more than tax-avoidance dodges.

WAYS FORWARD

Clearly there are many problems and disagreements. How might they be tackled? Part III of this study examines a variety of possible changes ranging from a completely new start to minor changes in administrative procedure. Specific recommendations have been deliberately avoided; the aim has been rather to identify and analyse the key areas of friction and, in each case, to put forward a *range* of options for change – in short, to provide an agenda for discussion.

Rational discussion of charity law is essential. There is great variety of opinion. Before any real progress can be made, charities, voluntary organisations and other interested parties need to debate among themselves just how far they feel it right to go. Little is likely to change without at least a degree of consensus and solidarity about what changes are needed.

Discussion is also important because knowledge of the law governing charities is not widespread. The limited understanding of the law and its administration among existing and would-be charities was one of the most striking aspects of the consultations undertaken in preparing this study. Rightly or wrongly, however, ignorance of the law is no excuse so there is a real need to raise the level of understanding.

CAVEAT EMPTOR

This book is not intended as a practical guide to the maze of rules, regulations and procedures through which existing and would-be charities must pick their way – a number of excellent publications already meet that need.[16] Nor does it attempt to analyse the whole question of tax concessions and other charitable privileges. If charitable status did not confer considerable tax advantages, the law of charity would, of course, be considerably less controversial and to that extent the issue is considered here; but the merits of different approaches to tax concessions are not immediately relevant.

The present writer is neither lawyer nor historian nor theologian and must apologise in advance for any mistakes or misunderstandings such a lack of professionalism may entail. Nevertheless a brief but systematic survey of the problems thrown up by the contemporary law of charity, and the possible solutions, has been found necessary for the purposes of the recently established Charity Law Working Group and it was felt that its publication might also help a little to inform the wider debate. This study aspires to the status of a 'reasoned memorandum' although it does not presume to advocate any particular changes; others, it is hoped, will improve its reasoning and co-operate in achieving every change that would enhance the overall 'public benefit' of the impact of charity law.

I. The Concept of Charity

1. Let My People Go

So long as democracy exists, even in its very imperfect English form, totalitarianism is in deadly danger. The whole English-speaking world is haunted by the idea of human equality, and . . . from the English-speaking culture, if it does not perish, a society of free and equal human beings will ultimately arise. But it is precisely the idea of human equality – the 'Jewish' or 'Judaeo-Christian' idea of equality – that Hitler came into the world to destroy. He has, heaven knows, said so often enough. The thought of a world in which black men would be as good as white men and Jews treated as human beings brings him the same horror and despair as the thought of endless slavery brings to us.

(George Orwell, 1941)[1]

The concept of charity has a long history. The word derives from the Latin *caritas*, itself a translation of the Greek *agape*. *Agape*, in turn, was the word chosen by the first translators of the Old Testament, around 200 BC, to represent the Hebrew *'hab*, 'love'. By origin, *'hab* signified erotic love but over time the word acquired a much wider range of meaning although it always retained 'the passionate overtones of complete engagement of the will accompanied by strong emotion'.[2]

A THEOLOGY OF LIBERATION

'Hab in the sense of 'love' or 'charity' was not a feature of early Jewish theology. All the evidence confirms that Moses never used the word, or anything resembling it; but his theology is important to an understanding of why the concept became increasingly important some four centuries later.

According to tradition, Moses was brought up at the Egyptian Court; certainly his name is Egyptian. Quite how and when the

9

Hebrew people settled in Egypt is far from clear but there is little doubt that by Moses' time, around 1300 BC, they had been in Egypt for several generations.

This was the Egypt of the New Empire. A rich and powerful nation, its sphere of influence extended as far north as Syria and its glittering civilisation produced such treasures as those found in the tomb of Tutankhamun. Politically, Egypt resembled the pyramids built some 1500 years earlier: at the pinnacle was the Pharaoh, the divine king; next came the viziers high priests and generals; and so on, down to a broad base of peasantry and, below even them, the slaves. It was not a closed society – able men could work their way up from the most humble beginnings to the highest offices of state; but it was profoundly hierarchical and bureaucratic.

Over the centuries Egypt had developed a strong moral code founded on the concept of *Maat* and although there is no adequate equivalent of the word in English,[3] in the ethical context the nearest translation is 'justice'. Professor Frankfort has emphasised its central importance in Egyptian thought:[4]

> Maat ... in the sense of social justice (means) righteous dealing with one's fellow-men ... the seeking out of good in relation to need: ferrying across the river the poor man who could not pay and doing good in advance of any known return. And ... social responsibility: the king was a herdsman who cherished his herds; the official had a positive duty towards the widow and orphan; in short, every man had rights which imposed responsibilities upon other men.

If it is true that Moses grew up at the Egyptian court, his outlook must have been deeply affected by such values. Certainly it would help to explain why Moses is said to have reacted so violently to encountering one of his people being beaten up by an Egyptian overseer, his sympathy for their down-trodden plight and his eventual plea to the Pharaoh, 'Let my people go'.

The Exodus story does not need recounting here but its theological consequences are significant. For Moses, the liberation of his people from slavery in Egypt was the work of Yahweh, the God who had commanded his return from exile in Arabia. And Yahweh's continuing protection had a price: obedience to his will. This was first and foremost a religious matter: monotheism – 'I am the Lord your God, who brought you out of Egypt, out of the land of slavery; you shall have no other gods'[5] – and the prohibition of idols and blasphemy. But ethical behaviour was also crucial; more than half the Ten Commandments were ethical rules and the wider Mosaic Law placed considerable emphasis on social justice, e.g.:

> You shall not ill-treat any widow or fatherless child. If you do . . . my anger will be roused and I will kill you with the sword. . . . You shall not deprive the poor man of justice. . . . You shall not oppress the alien, for you know how it feels to be an alien; you were aliens yourselves in Egypt.[6]

The Jewish people had found freedom; but the price of liberation was monotheism, righteousness and social justice.

THE SNARE OF KINGSHIP

In fact, the social conduct prescribed by the Mosaic Law did not differ greatly from the traditional Egyptian values. But unlike Egypt, the Hebrews, once settled in Palestine, rejected the whole institution of kingship and centralised power. *Their* Lord was Yahweh and this appears to have promoted democratic and egalitarian attitudes. For over 200 years, Israel relied upon a tribal, decentralised polity with no bureaucracy. Its economy was agricultural and pastoral, class distinctions were absent and commerce and urban life rudimentary.

But during the eleventh century the loose, decentralised league of Twelve Tribes came under increasing pressure from the Philistines. Under Samuel, the last of the judges, the threat was held at bay but when he grew old the people asked him to 'appoint us a king to govern us, like other nations'. In the end, Samuel reluctantly agreed but not without a solemn warning:

> This will be the manner of king that will reign over you. He will take your sons and make them serve in his chariots and with his cavalry. . . . Others will plough his fields and reap his harvest. He will take your daughters for perfumers, cooks and confectioners, and will seize the best of your cornfields, vineyards and olive-yards, and give them to his lackeys. . . . He will take a tenth of your flocks, and you yourselves will become his slaves. When that day comes you will cry out against the king whom you have chosen; but it will be too late.[7]

Samuel's predictions were not far off the mark. After Saul's brief and uneven reign David came to the throne and using mercenaries established a major Palestinian state including much of Syria. His son, Solomon, was an able diplomat and administrator who established a centralised state and labour services and a standing army. Even so, he lost half the territorial gains his father had made and, after his death in 926 BC, the kingdom split in two – a southern kingdom known as Judah and a northern kingdom called Israel.

Half a century later, a military coup put Omri on the northern throne. His successor Ahab married a Phoenician princess, Jezebel, and soon Phoenician deities were introduced and worshipped. This threat to monotheism was challenged by the first of the great prophets, Elijah, who led a popular rising which eventually deposed the 'House of Omri' and suppressed the cult of Baal. But Jehu, who next assumed the throne, proved equally unsatisfactory. He butchered political opponents wholesale and reintroduced the cult of the golden calf. And so it went on.

The rise of the prophets was intimately connected with the introduction of kingship. Before that it was believed that Yahweh ruled his people directly by selecting and empowering key individuals as leaders. Now, however, a king would become the national leader not because of his charismatic gifts but because he had the proper father. Prophecy preserved the older tradition:

> No matter how great the king's political power, the prophet as God's spokesman was always at hand to say 'Thus saith the Lord' to any being or to the people as a whole when they went contrary to the old Mosaic covenant. As a result, there could be no real curb on freedom of speech in ancient Israel.[8]

The Hebrew word for prophet, *nabi*, means 'he who is called' and the prophets were not primarily futurologists though some of their predictions were extremely accurate; as has been aptly said, they were forthtellers rather than foretellers.

In the eighth century BC a new breed of prophets appeared – the literary prophets, so called because they were the first whose words were preserved and written down in books bearing their names. But the title is justified on another score: they were poets who proclaimed their message of ethical, social and political criticism in verse as well as prose.

POETS OF REFORM

The eighth century was a time of rapid economic and social change. The monarchy had weakened the old tribal structure by dividing the country into new districts created for purely administrative purposes and from the beginning the kings created a new class of landowners by rewarding their more loyal subjects with gifts of land and other benefits. With rapid urbanisation, barter gave way to a money economy and many of the peasants became financially dependent on townsmen. All this was exacerbated by chronic warfare which tended to polarise society between the wealthy few, who profited from war, and the masses whom it impoverished. Under these pressures, the relative social and economic equality of the old tribal system gradually crumbled away.

Idolatry had long been denounced on the grounds that it would lose the nation Yahweh's support. But the literary prophets were the first to preach that disobeying his demands for social justice was equally perilous. This led them to become practical moralists, politicians and jurists, resolved to do all they could to uproot social evil. They stopped short only at revolution – 'notwithstanding the frequent and often harsh criticism directed against particular monarchs by the prophets, they were never ready to back up violent actions'[9] – and so were the first to draw a line which remains one of the principal boundaries of free speech in the law of modern democracies.

Their political activity was grounded, however, in a devout piety; they saw their elevated and often beautiful poetry as inspired by Yahweh. Often they spoke in his name and, as a leading Old Testament scholar put it: 'The whole form of their preaching, with its "Thus saith the Lord" represents the prophet as nothing more than the speaking tube of a higher power.'[10]

The first of the classical prophets was Amos who was active around 750 BC. Amos ignored idolatry – his target was social injustice. He rose above the view that attributes poverty to individual fecklessness; it was the wealthy and the noble who 'grind the heads of the poor in the dust/and thrust the humble out of their way'.[11] And through Amos came dire threats:

> Listen to this . . .
> you who oppress the poor
> and crush the destitute

> . . . your time is coming.
> You that turn justice upside down
> and bring righteousness to the ground . . .
> for all this, because you levy taxes on the poor
> and extort a tribute of grain from them,
> though you have built houses of hewn stone,
> you shall not live in them,
> though you have planted pleasant vineyards,
> you shall not drink wine from them. . . .
> Behold, I the Lord God
> have my eyes on this sinful kingdom
> and I will wipe it off the face of the earth.[12]

Avoidance of idolatry was not enough; even religious worship, if unaccompanied by social justice, was unacceptable:

> I hate, I spurn your pilgrim-feasts;
> I will not delight in your sacred ceremonies.
> When you present your sacrifices and offerings
> I will not accept them. . . .
> Spare me the sound of your songs;
> I cannot endure the music of your lutes. Rather,
> let justice roll on like a river
> and righteousness like an ever-flowing stream.[13]

Twenty years later Hosea appeared on the scene. Like Amos he preached impending disaster and the need to repent and 'practise justice'.[14] But he went beyond Amos, in two respects. He bitterly attacked the monarchy and its foreign policy:

> What use is a king to us?
> There is nothing but talk,
> imposing of oaths
> and making of treaties,
> all to no purpose.[15]

And he introduced the vocabulary of love into classical prophecy, an innovation that seems to have its roots in his own personal experience.

Little is known about Hosea's life apart from his marriage and the precise character even of that troubled relationship remains obscure. Hosea tells us that Yahweh instructed him to marry a loose woman by the name of Gomer: 'Go, take a wanton for your wife and get children of her wantoness; for like a wanton this land is unfaithful to the Lord'.[16] It is not clear, however, whether

14

Gomer deserted him or whether he divorced her for adultery but it seems that eventually she ended in slavery. At any rate, Hosea was instructed to buy her freedom and take her back.

There are other possible interpretations of the texts but the detail is unimportant: the central element of the relationship – the love and mercy shown by the husband towards his unfaithful wife – became, for Hosea, a powerful metaphor for Yahweh's attitude to his people. This was a daring step; the word '*hab* (love) was redolent of the fertility rites and sacred prostitution of the pagan religions. But like many another striking act by which the prophets sought to attract the attention of the people[17] it enabled Hosea to dramatise his message.

The disaster predicted by Amos and Hosea soon struck. In 722 BC, after a three-year siege, the Assyrian emperor Sargon II destroyed the northern kingdom. Many of the Israelites were deported and Israel became an Assyrian province.

But prophecy did not die out. The southern kingdom, Judah, survived, although for years it was forced to pay tribute to Damascus. Its survival was partly due to the great prophet and shrewd politician, Isaiah. As with Hosea, Isaiah's preaching was sharply critical of the monarchical system:

> Your very rulers are rebels,
> confederate with thieves;
> every man of them loves a bribe
> and itches for a gift.[18]

and as with Amos, it puts social justice before religious worship:

> When you lift your hands
> outspread in prayer
> I shall hide my eyes from you.
> Though you offer countless prayers
> I shall not listen.
> There is blood on your hands:
> wash you, make you clean;
> put away the evil of your deeds
> away out of my sight.
> Cease to do evil, learn to do right
> pursue justice, champion the oppressed
> give the orphan his rights,
> plead the widow's cause.[19]

But Isaiah shows little trace of the new metaphor of love. Nor were his predictions of disaster fulfilled, at least, not immediately.

A NEW COVENANT

Half a century after Isaiah the pious young Josiah came to the throne of Judah and sponsored a general religious reformation. During renovation of the Temple an ancient scroll was discovered; suitably edited and amplified, the book of Deuteronomy (as it is known today) became the basis of a revival of Mosaic law.

Deuteronomy shows the marked influence of Hosea's preaching. It makes extensive use of the vocabulary of love; and whereas Hosea had baulked at referring to human love for Yahweh (he preferred to speak of knowledge or loyalty), the Deuteronomists knew no such inhibition: 'Thou shalt love the Lord thy God with all thy heart. . . .'[20]

But their real innovation was the 'contract' language of the covenant. It is doubtful whether the formal covenant they attributed to the Mosaic era ever took place but the idea of a contract of this kind between Yahweh and his people was central to the new message. A Deuteronomist passage[21] relates that 'Moses wrote down all the words of the Lord' and after slaughtering a number of bulls, assembled the people:

> Moses took half the blood and put it into basins and the other half he flung against the altar. Then he took the book of the covenant and read it aloud for all the people to hear. They said, 'We will obey, and do all that the Lord has said'. Moses then took the blood and flung it over the people, saying, 'This is the blood of the covenant which the Lord has made with you on the terms of this book'.

In spelling out the terms of the covenant, Deuteronomy introduces a number of new themes. It offers a plan of social reform with new rules for the protection of the poor.[22] It marks the beginning of a new attitude towards slavery, e.g.:

> You shall not surrender to his master a slave who takes refuge with you. Let him stay with you anywhere he chooses ... wherever suits him best; you shall not force him.[23]

This is in marked contrast with Greece or the old Babylonian law: 'He who hides an escaped slave must be put to death'.[24] And Deuteronomy even introduces a number of laws against cruelty to animals.[25]

By the end of Josiah's reign, however, a new cloud appeared on the horizon. In 610 BC the rising power of Babylon defeated the Assyrians and by 597 BC the Babylonian armies entered Jerusalem. Heedless of the warnings of the prophet Jeremiah, the new king Zedekiah persisted in plotting revolts, relying – against all experience – on Egyptian support. Jeremiah, who advocated submission to Babylon and was imprisoned for demoralising the populace, was proved right. In 587 BC came the destruction of Jerusalem and the deportation of half the population to Babylonia.

Apart from his unpopular views on foreign policy, Jeremiah followed the tradition of the earlier prophets, denouncing injustice and the monarchy[26] and employing the Hosean imagery of love and marriage.[27] But whereas it was the Deuteronomists who gave the vocabulary of love a lasting place in Jewish theology, it was Jeremiah who first wrestled with the theological implications of Hosea's innovation. He recognised the dangers of covenant theology, in particular, the ease with which a legalistic interpretation of outward codes of behaviour can, by conforming with the letter of the law but ignoring its spirit, circumvent social justice. Whereas Moses' liberation theology had laid down that the price of freedom was social justice, Jeremiah came to see that justice could not be compelled merely by laws but depended on a change of heart:

> The time is coming, says the Lord, when I will make a new covenant with Israel and Judah. It will not be like the covenant I made with their forefathers ... But this is the covenant which I will make ... I will set my law within them and write in on their hearts.[28]

Exiled in Babylon, others took up the theme. The second Isaiah spoke of Yahweh's break with the past:

> Cease to dwell on days gone by
> And to brood over past history;
> Here and now I will do a new thing
> This moment it will break into bud
> Can you not perceive it?[29]

The prophet Ezekiel, too, proclaimed the new message: 'I will give you a new heart and put a new spirit within you; I will remove the stony heart from your body and give you a heart of flesh'.[30] But it was the anonymous writers of the 'priestly school' who took the final step in the development of Hosea's preaching and proclaimed: 'Thou shalt love thy neighbour as thyself'.[31]

THE SECOND COMMOMWEALTH

It was half a century before a new imperialism ended the Babylonian exile. In 539 BC Cyrus II of Persia conquered Babylon; by 525 BC the Persian empire stretched right down into Egypt. Cyrus allowed the Jews to return to Palestine but it was not until 444 BC that the Persian king Artaxerxes granted a charter to Ezra – a scholar and priest raised in Babylon – empowering him to enforce the Mosaic code as the imperial law for the Jews in Palestine. Under Persian suzerainty, Ezra and his circle rebuilt Israel as a theocratic state governed not by kings but by the Torah – the traditional law – administered by scribes and their successors, the Pharisees and rabbis. The Temple was rebuilt and the new emphasis on law and cult marked the end of the age of prophecy.

Overlords came and went but the Torah governed the Jews in Palestine for a further six centuries. In 332 BC Alexander the Great swept away the Persians and in 63 BC Pompey incorporated Palestine into the Roman empire. After an uprising in AD 66, Vespasian destroyed Jerusalem and a further revolt in AD 133 led Hadrian to disperse the Jewish people and suppress the teaching and practice of the Jewish Torah. By this time the theology of love was firmly established. Rabbi Akiba, one of the principal founders of modern Judaism, taught that 'The fundamental principle of the Torah is the commandment, Love they neighbour as thyself'.[37]

MERCY AND JUSTICE

This brief survey of the evolution of the concept of charity, in its Jewish phase, has of necessity presented a highly selective account of the complex themes of Jewish theology. But it should suffice to show that love (charity) became – and remains – central to Jewish belief.

This concept of love is not simply a matter of mercy and benevolence. Charity, in the Jewish view, cannot ignore injustice.

Despise not the Lord's rebuke
Nor be weary of his correction;
For whom he loves, the Lord chastises,
As a father, the son in whom he delights.[33]

Thus the prophetic vision saw justice and mercy as the twin pillars of ethical conduct. Hence the prophets' political engagement; for, where necessary, love implies social criticism. And this is, no doubt, as it should be; for although the arrogant may resent even justified reproach:

Rebuke a wise man
And he will love you.[34]

2. Agape and Koinonia

*Though I speak with the tongues
of men and of angels, and
have not charity, I am
become as sounding brass
or a tinkling cymbal.
And though I have the gift of
prophecy, and understand all
mysteries, and all knowledge;
and though I have all faith,
so that I could remove
mountains, and have not
charity, I am nothing.
And though I bestow all my goods
to feed the poor, and though I
give my body to be burned,
and have not charity, it
profiteth me nothing.*

(St Paul)[1]

It seems, then, that the concept of charity was born and developed out of the Jewish prophets' relentless campaigning against social, economic and political injustice and from their attempts to bring pressure to bear on the governments of their time to procure changes in policies and administrative practices. But the main channel through which the concept of charity came to exercise its lasting influence on the western world was the Christian religion, and this chapter attempts a brief sketch of how this came about. Again, this must of necessity be a highly selective account, concentrating almost entirely on the development of the concept of charity and ignoring any wider issues of Christian theology.

The Christian religion derives its title from the Greek word *Christos* in translation from the Hebrew *mashiach*, 'messiah'. The word means 'anointed' and refers to the ancient Jewish practice of anointing kings and high priests with oil at the time of their installation in office. After the Babylonian exile the decline of the prophetic movement was paralleled by the rise of apocalyptic thought which included the belief that at some unspecified time a messiah would appear. The dominant conception of this messiah seems to have been monarchic:[2] a king who would lead a successful military uprising, restore the kingdom of Israel and thereafter 'judge the poor with justice, and defend the humble'.[3]

Clearly Jesus was not a figure of this kind, and the general consensus of New Testament scholars is that he consistently refused to accept any of the messianic titles.[4] Still less did he see himself as divine. 'Son of God', and the related filial vocabulary he used, was no innovation[5] but deeply rooted in Old Testament tradition going back to the imagery of Hosea, as described earlier. It indicated not metaphysical origin or exalted status but vocation and obedience.

THE SUFFERING SERVANT

More than anything else, Jesus himself seems to have conceived of his role as that of a prophet. He frequently describes himself as such and his sayings are full of allusions to the classical prophets.

There were, in fact, two strands in Jewish apocalyptic teaching. Besides the popular expectation of a warrior king, another tradition foresaw a very different figure, most vividly characterised in the prophecy of the Second Isaiah. In line with prophetic tradition, justice and mercy are what is crucial and they will be best served, not by a king, but a servant. Second Isaiah, however, universalises the message: the servant will bring justice to all nations,[6] not just the Jews:

> He will make justice shine on every race,
> never faltering, never breaking down,
> he will plant justice on earth
> while coasts and islands wait for his teaching.[7]

Later Isaiah goes on to describe the suffering this servant would have to endure:

> He was despised and rejected of men,
> A man of sorrows and acquainted with grief...
> He was oppressed and afflicted,
> Yet he opened not his mouth;
> Brought as a lamb to the slaughter...
> Without protection, without justice...
> He was cut off from the land of the living.[8]

This vicarious suffering is not for nothing: it will usher in the new age of love and mercy[9] while the 'servant' will be vindicated and counted among the great.[10]

There seems little doubt that Jesus modelled himself on the suffering servant. He announced his 'mission' by quoting another passage from Isaiah:

> The Lord has anointed me;
> He has sent me to bring good news to the poor
> To bind up the broken-hearted,
> To proclaim liberty to captives
> And release to those in prison.[11]

and proceeded to act out every detail of the daunting role Isaiah had prescribed.

THE LEGACY OF THE PROPHETS

In reviving the tradition of the prophets Jesus did not seek to alter or add to their message. Like them, he urged repentance, love and social justice. Jesus' originality lay not in *what* he said but *how* he said it, in the power and range of his poetic imagination: the vivid imagery, striking parables, and quick retorts to awkward questions; and in the way he revived the dramatising bent of the prophets, the use of striking symbolic actions as a means of arresting the attention of the people.

The purpose of all this was, of course, to renew and implement the prophets' conception of a new covenant, a 'New Deal' by which love, mercy and justice would be written in people's hearts not merely in their laws. Hence the final evocative gesture: to accept judicial murder as the means of sealing the New Deal. For just as Moses was said to have sealed the original covenant with the blood of bulls, Jesus saw himself as Isaiah's 'lamb to the slaughter', perishing to provide 'the blood of the new covenant'.[12]

SERVICE AND PROTEST

The relief of poverty and other afflictions was to be a central feature of the New Deal. To illustrate this message Jesus chose a life of absolute poverty, renouncing possessions and family ties, and expected his followers to do the same. Feeding the hungry, healing the sick and teaching the ignorant, he moved among the lowest strata of society, constantly affirming his solidarity with the poor and with social outcasts such as tax-collectors and prostitutes. He did not favour violent attempts at political change, partly perhaps because he recognised the hopelessness of challenging the might of imperial Rome but more probably because, following Jeremiah and his successors, he doubted that political change without a change of heart can bring about a just society.

To speak as some have, however, of Jesus' political disengagement and respect for established authority seems very wide of the mark. Contempt for private property, rejection of family ties and condemnation of the cash-nexus are hardly the mark of one who accepts the *status quo*. But Jesus' political engagement was the 'direct action' of the libertarian not the 'vanguard' politics of the authoritarian socialist. Direct action in the shape of his disciples' *community of possessions* with its common purse. Direct action in the form of *service* to anyone and everyone in need, a duty incompatible with love of money ('no one can serve two masters') or desire for power:

> Throughout the world, kings lord it over their subjects; and those in authority are called their country's 'Benefactors' – But you shall not be so: the highest among you must behave like the most junior, the chief of you like a servant.[13]

And direct action in the form of *protest*: sometimes practical – driving the money lenders out of the Temple or intervening to save an adulteress from stoning – and sometimes a searing critique of established authority. So, for example, towards the end, addressing a crowd in Jerusalem, Jesus throws all caution to the wind:

> The lawyers and the Pharisees sit in the chair of Moses; therefore do what they tell you . . . but do not follow their practice, for they say one thing and do another . . .
> Woe unto you, lawyers and Pharisees, hypocrites. You pay tithes of mint and dill and cummin; but you have ignored the weightier demands of the law, justice, mercy and good faith. It is these you should have practised . . . Blind guides! You strain out a gnat and swallow a camel.
> Woe unto you, lawyers and Pharisees, hypocrites. You are like white washed tombs, which look well from the outside, but inside are full of dead men's bones . . .[14]

THE COMMON LIFE

The influence of these radical views on western political thought continues even today, although their origins are often unrecognised. Their impact in the early days of the church in Jerusalem is well known, however:

> All who had become believers held everything in common; they would sell their property and possessions so as to distribute to each according to their need. With one mind they kept up their daily attendance at the Temple, and, breaking bread in private houses, shared their meals with unaffected joy . . .[15]

In the original Greek, this primitive communism is described as *koinonia*. The word is derived from *koinos*, common, and its literal meaning is 'sharing' – having or giving a share; but since what was shared was a great deal more than just material possessions, *koinonia* is generally translated as 'fellowship' or 'the common life'. *Koinonia* was understood as the outward sign of *agape* (love), the central pivot of Jesus' proclamation; and its fundamental meaning neatly captures the sense in which charity reaches out towards social justice, as much in Christian as in Jewish ethics. And although Jesus may not have *taught* anything very original, his dramatic career had inspired a radically new attempt to *implement* the prophets' message.

The subsequent development of this early *koinonia* is usefully illumined by Victor Turner in his seminal work, *The Ritual Process*.[16] An anthropologist, Professor Turner begins from an analysis of 'rites of passage' in primitive societies, such as puberty rites, or the ceremonies installing tribal elders. Following Van Gennep,[17] he notes that all such rites of transition are marked by three phases: *separation*, symbolic detachment of the individual or group from the previous status; *margin*, an intervening 'threshold' phase; and *reaggregation*, return to everyday life with a new status.

Turner focuses on the characteristics of the intervening 'threshold phase', for which he coins the word 'communitas'. Stripped of their previous status, the ritual participants enter a state of 'lowliness and sacredness, homogeneity and comradeship, a generalised social bond . . . yet to be fragmented into a multiplicity of social ties'. Turner goes on to contrast 'communitas' with the 'status system' of everyday life:

> It is as though there are here two major 'models' for human interrelatedness, juxtaposed and alternating. The first is of society as a structured, differentiated and often hierarchical

system of politico-legal-economic positions with many types of evaluation, separating men in terms of 'more' or 'less' . . . [18]

The second model, 'communitas', involves 'a relationship between concrete, historical, idiosyncratic individuals . . . not segmentalised into roles and statuses' but a 'direct, immediate and total confrontation of human identities'.

But Turner questions whether *permanent* communitas is possible or practical as a basis for social life in general:

> The spontaneity and immediacy of communitas . . . can seldom be maintained for very long. Communitas itself soon develops a structure, in which free relationships between individuals become converted into norm-governed relationships between social personae . . . It is the fate of all spontaneous communitas to undergo what most people see as a 'decline and fall' into structure and law. [19]

And while he acknowledges the compelling attraction of communitas, Turner questions the wisdom of attempting to make it the exclusive basis of social life:

> For many millenarian and 'enthusiastic' movements . . . the ecstasy of spontaneous communitas is seen as *the* end of human endeavour. In the religion of pre-industrial societies, this state is regarded rather as a means to the end of becoming more fully involved in the rich manifold of structural role-playing. In this there is perhaps a greater wisdom, for human beings are responsible to one another in the supplying of humble needs, such as food, drink, clothing, and the careful teaching of material and social techniques.
>
> Social structure . . . is not merely the set of chains in which men everywhere are, but the very cultural means that preserve the dignity and liberty, as well as the bodily existence, of every man, woman and child. [20]

But in practice, as Turner admits, wisdom is not always readily found; the balance between structure and communitas is not easy to maintain and the chains often become oppressive. Hence the repeated upsurge of communitas, whether it be Solidarity in Poland, the current travails of the British Labour Party or the *koinonia* of the earliest church.

AGAPE AND LAW

The apostles themselves seem to have been aware that communitas, however excellent in itself, like a soufflé may not have staying power. As numbers grew, disputes broke out, with the Greek-speaking believers complaining that their widows were being overlooked in the daily distribution. To deal with this the whole body of believers were told to elect 'seven men of good reputation' as *diakonoi* (deacons) to organise the material aspect of the *koinonia*.[21] This democratic move, the creation of an elected Diaconate, was the first step in a long process of institutionalisation leading in time to the whole episcopal hierarchy of bishops, priests, deacons and the like.

St Paul, an inveterate organiser, contributed in some respects to this trend, being always distinctly suspicious of unrestrained communitas. But his missionary zeal for the conversion of the Gentile world had a markedly opposite effect. The earliest Christians were almost all Jewish and continued to adhere to the Mosaic legal tradition so that Paul's activities soon raised the question of whether anyone could join the new Church without submitting to Jewish Law. After some controversy, Paul had his way and this averted what would otherwise have probably been the fate of the early Christian communitas: to be quickly reabsorbed by the highly structured Jewish way of life.

Theologically, Paul buttressed his position by building on the line of thought begun by Jeremiah. A new covenant has been established 'written not on tablets of stone but on the pages of the human heart'[22] and the believers 'are discharged from the law . . . the old way, the way of a written code'.[23] Not that the old way was intrinsically wrong but people had ignored the spirit and purpose of the law, obeying only the letter, if that, whereas 'the letter killeth but the spirit giveth life'.[24]

The new covenant cannot be expressed in a written code. It is a question of a fundamental attitude, *agape*, from which the right conduct will flow without the need of rules and regulations, for 'He who loves his neighbour has fulfilled the law'.[25] By stressing that the new dispensation was founded on a fundamental change of heart, Paul individualised *koinonia*, detaching it from its social setting and rooting it in the inner attitude of the individual believer. His repeated contrast of *agape* and law – aptly summarised by Augustine as 'Love and do what you will' –

inoculated Christian belief against any permanent structural fossilisation and provided the cue for many a revival of the spontaneous communitas or *koinonia* of the earliest church. And his insistence on the centrality of *agape* led subsequent theologians to the progressive apotheosis of love, reaching its culmination in the assertion that *agape is* the God of the Christians: 'Dear friends, let us love one another, for God is love'[26] or, as Wycliffe originally translated it: 'God is charitie'.

CHURCH AND EMPIRE

Despite frequent persecutions, the new religion spread rapidly across the Roman Empire and *koinonia* seems to have played an important part in this:

> The practical application of charity was probably the most potent single cause of Christian success. The pagan comment 'See how these Christians love one another' . . . was not irony. Christian charity expressed itself in care for the poor, for widows and orphans, in visits to brethren in prison or condemned to the living death of labour in the mines, and in social action in time of calamity like famine, earthquake, pestilence, or war . . . But the distribution of alms was not confined only to believers (and) the assistance provided by the church was impressive in a world where . . . the government did not expect to undertake a general programme of social welfare.[27]

By the end of the third century Christianity was widely disseminated in society throughout the empire. Sporadic persecutions continued until the 'conversion' of the emperor Constantine around AD 311. On one view,[28] Constantine never really became a Christian but used the religion for his own political purposes, displacing Christian ethics with those of his own imperial ideology with disastrous results for the integrity of the church. There is more than a grain of truth in this but it is not the whole story. He supported the church's practical work by assigning 'a fixed proportion of provincial revenues to church charity, so large that even when cut to a third', some fifty years later, 'it was reckoned generous'.[29] Constantine also endeavoured to express Christian ideals in some of his laws, protecting children, slaves, peasants and prisoners.

Although Constantine favoured Christianity among the

many religions of his empire he never made it the official, state religion. That 'nationalisation' of the church did not come about until half a century after his death when Ambrose, the astute bishop of Milan, established a decisive influence over the emperor Theodosius. From then on church and state were to become inextricably interlinked.

MEDIEVAL CHARITY

By this time, however, the state itself was crumbling under the impact of wave after wave of barbarian invasion and before long the empire fragmented into a variety of separately governed states. In the East the Byzantine empire persisted for centuries longer, but in the West civilisation slowly disintegrated.

The church survived, however, gradually converting the invaders and, in the monasteries, keeping alive some of the literacy and scholarship of the fading ancient world. Monasticism had its roots in early attempts to revive the 'common life' of the earliest church and, taking vows of poverty, the monks worked to create islands of *koinonia* within a church drained of 'communitas' by progressive institutionalisation. But the monastic orders themselves were not immune to the natural tendency to routinise *koinonia*; over and again, during the Middle Ages, new orders were brought into being by those who wished to return to the spontaneity of 'communitas', and old orders were reformed and reinvigorated.

The monasteries were centres of practical charity, relieving poverty, tending the sick and the old and providing education. But they were not the only way medieval society met the needs of the poor and others in need. The local churches, under the bishops, raised tithes part of which were distributed to those in need; the feudal landlords were expected to look to the welfare of their tenants; and in the towns, burghers and guilds gradually established secular alternatives to the almshouses, hospitals and schools of the monasteries.

There were, as is well known, many abuses in the medieval church and the wealth and power of the ecclesiastical hierarchy attracted increasing criticism. Men like John Wycliffe began to urge the cause of radical reform, arguing that the church should give up its possessions and return to the original *koinonia*. Popular discontent simmered away, occasionally erupting in violent action like the Peasants' Revolt of 1381, sparked off by John Ball's revolutionary sermon on the text:

> When Adam delved and Eve span,
> Who then was the gentleman?

But radical changes did not come until early in the sixteenth century when Martin Luther, beginning in 1517, launched a passionate protest at the shortcomings of the church. His object was the reform of the doctrines and practices of the Roman Church but the outcome was the birth of the Protestant churches. *Protest* – in the sense of dissent – was of the essence of the Reformation and once begun the tide of protest proved hard to check. The original Protestant Churches found themselves challenged in turn by more radical dissenters and, in time, even Nonconformist radicalism was outflanked by secular political movements – 'broad' and narrow 'churches' which often still appear to hanker after the spontaneous communitas of the earliest *koinonia*.

Among the changes brought by the Reformation was a gradual divergence of the various meanings of the word 'charity'. In popular usage the word has become more or less equivalent to alms-giving, sometimes even with a derogatory flavour, as in a recent advertisement which reads:

> Through Action Aid sponsorship, you can give a child much more than charity. You can give a child a real chance to help himself. To grow food or learn a skill to support his family. Ultimately, to make a more secure life, both for himself and his community.[30]

In legal use, the term has a broader, albeit specialised and at times rather surprising, range of meaning and the process by which this came about is the subject of the next chapter.

In theological use, however, the term has stayed relatively close to its origins and a brief sketch of contemporary perspectives on charity may be of interest.

AGAPE AND JUSTICE IN CONTEMPORARY THOUGHT

Modern philosophers and theologians have created an extensive literature on the subject of *agape* and space does not permit a detailed account of the diversity of views they have expressed. The American philosopher, Gene Outka, has provided a helpful systematic survey of the field[31] and the following account attempts no more than to summarise his conclusions.

A close analysis of the injunction to 'love your neighbour as yourself' and the context in which it occurs leads to a definition of *agape* as essentially *equal and unconditional concern* for the interests of all one's fellow human beings (some would extend this to the animal and vegetable kingdoms as well). *Unconditional* concern implies both independence and stability. *Independence*, because the love in question does not arise from and is not affected by who or what the neighbour is, or as Karl Barth puts it, charity means 'identification with his interests in utter independence of the question of his attractiveness'.[32] *Stability*, because even if you disapprove of people's behaviour it is still possible to remain concerned about them. 'Love is not love, which alters when it alteration finds' as the famous sonnet says:

> Love's not Time's fool, though rosy lips and cheeks,
> Within his bending sickle's compass come;
> Love alters not with his brief hours and weeks,
> But bears it out, even to the edge of doom.[33]

The corollary to this unconditional concern is that, since every neighbour is included, a basic *equality* results 'whereby one neighbour's well-being is as valuable as another's ... At the most basic level there ought to be no exclusiveness, no partiality, no elitism'.[34]

Equal and unconditional concern does not, however, imply a blank cheque. Other things being equal, it is true that *agape* logically implies putting neighbours first if their interests conflict with yours, since to put yourself first would be to love them *less* then yourself. But this does not imply wholesale self-sacrifice. In the first place not everyone recognises their best interests, so that '*for the sake of the neighbour* one may have to resist his exploitation as well as attend to his needs'.[35] Secondly, there is the 'third-party' dilemma: as often as not, moral choices involve not merely a single neighbour but a range of others as well, whose interests must be taken into account. Finally, the range of *equal and unconditional concern* is all human beings and this extends to oneself, or as Kierkegaard observed: 'The law is therefore: you shall love yourself in the same way as you love your neighbour when you love him as yourself'.[36]

There is, of course, a line in contemporary thought which rejects the possibility of *agape* on the grounds that altruistic behaviour does not exist, that we never have any concern or desire for the welfare of others except as a means to our own. No one can deny that some apparently altruistic behaviour is, in reality, selfishly motivated. But to see all such behaviour as aiming at self-gratification is implausible: counter-examples abound, such as the fireman who returns repeatedly, beyond the call of duty, to rescue those trapped in a blazing building. To say that this was done for the praise or glory or gratitude that may accrue after the event (supposing the man survives) is to confuse motive with outcome.

Finally, a persistent theme in contemporary discussion is the relationship between *agape* and justice. The issue is bedevilled, however, by a constant failure to distinguish among various quite different conceptions of justice. Hence while some writers, such as Anders Nygren,[37] have concluded that *agape* is incompatible with justice, others have seen the two concepts as interchangeable, as, for example, Joseph Fletcher, who writes: 'Love and justice are the same, for justice is love distributed, nothing else'.[38] Most scholars, however, have taken a middle position, distinguishing the two conceptions but seeing a substantial area of overlap. Gene Outka belongs to this last category. He carefully distinguishes a number of views of justice pointing out that this enables one to reconcile most of the apparently conflicting views.

If justice is taken to mean *to each according to his merit*, Nygren's view must prevail. On the merit principle,

> Justice is ... a grading concept in terms of which various achievements and acquired characteristics are assessed. High marks are given because or insofar as someone has done something meritorious. Advantages are allocated in accordance with particular conduct and not because the several parties are all human beings. (But) the value which agape attaches to each man prior to his doing anything in particular is obviously never reducible to any such grading criterion. Agape prohibits us from grading persons as such. They ought never to be valued only for their merits.[39]

But 'reward proportioned to merit' is not the only prevalent conception of justice. A more egalitarian view sees justice as *to each the same thing.* Here the underlying distributive principle is not merit but some conception of fundamental human rights with everyone entitled to basic necessities and freedoms, irrespective of their capacity or contribution to the general good (although misconduct may, on this view, necessitate some curtailment of entitlement). This version of justice is much closer to the *equal and unconditional concern* of *agape*, with its corollary of respect for the irreducible worth and dignity of every fellow human being. But there are differences:

> Agape prohibits discriminatory judgements where these determine whether the other is to be cared about at all, but it allows and may require that he be cared about appropriately . . . equal consideration is not the same as identical treatment.[40]

So, for example, as Outka goes on to point out: 'Traditionally agape has been thought to involve a rectifying bias towards the disadvantaged, handicapped and defenseless'.[41]

Still closer, therefore, is the conception of justice summed up in the phrase *to each according to need.* This version, the justice of *koinonia*,[42] is not, of course, to everyone's taste:

> A standard criticism of this formula is that it warrants only one kind of inequality and fails to provide for other sorts of relevant differences based on other sorts of claims. Claims of potential recipients differ not only in relation to need, but also in relation to special promises and contracts, special ties of kinship, etc. In a striking way, however, precisely the same kind of objection has been lodged against *agape*.[43]

So close to *agape* is justice, in the sense of *to each according to need,* that this version, *social* justice as opposed to the meritocratic variety, is generally seen as being implied, in every detail, by the principle 'love your neighbour as yourself'.

Nevertheless, charity or *equal and unconditional concern* is not exhausted by social justice, with its emphasis on needs. *Agape* is free, for example, to distinguish between needs and *preferences* and to hold that both count in the advancement of neighbours' well-being, although here, too, equalitarian premises, *equal* concern, will apply. And Outka argues that it is in your neighbours' interest to 'dispense praise unequally because one of the wants persons share equally is proportionate recognition of acquired excellences',[44] going on to quote Gregory Vlastos' observation that 'It would be sheer confusion to think that there would be any incompatibility between deciding to distribute praise according to merit and economic goods according to need'.[45]

But that said, it is clear that there is a deep conjunction between *agape* and *koinonia* such that charity must always strive towards social justice, however humble or inadequate the means at its disposal may be, and however irritating to those in positions of authority the methods it adopts.

3. Charity and Equity

In ordinary language 'equity' means natural justice; but the beginner must get the idea out of his head when dealing with the system that lawyers call equity. Originally, indeed, this system was inspired by ideas of natural justice, and that is why it acquired its name; but nowadays equity is no more (and no less) natural justice than the common law, and it is in fact nothing else than a particular branch of the law of England.

(Professor Glanville Williams)[1]

The greater part of equity is concerned with the law of trusts, of which charitable trusts form an important sub-section. Consequently the law relating to charities is primarily a matter of equity. The roots of equity go back to the Middle Ages, when the courts of common law failed to give redress in certain types of case where justice required redress. Among such cases were those involving breach of obligation in the carrying out of trusts or 'uses', as they were originally known.

ORIGINS OF THE TRUST

Every trust attempts to control the fate of some economic asset. Three parties are involved: the *settlor*, who provides both the asset and the terms on which it is made available; the *trustee* who holds the asset on those terms; and the *beneficiary* whose welfare is the object of the exercise. The trust is a uniquely English invention; continental legal systems, based on Roman law and Roman conceptions of property, have never favoured its principle of *dual ownership*: the separation of trustees' rights to administer property from beneficiaries' right to enjoy it.

The ancestor of the modern trust was the medieval 'use' but the exact origins of the 'use' are obscure. On one view the 'use' was an adaptation of a foreign concept, for although Roman law does not permit dual ownership it does allow that *dominium* (full ownership) may be limited by *jura in re aliena* (rights over another's property) among which are *usus* (use) and *ususfructus*. The usufruct confers a right to use and enjoy the fruits of another's property; the use is similar but excludes the right to fruits. These foreign notions played no part in the English common law of property but they did cross the channel during the thirteenth century for a different purpose.

In the years after 1205 a remarkable eruption of the spontaneous *communitas* discussed in the last chapter occurred, first in Italy but soon spreading to other countries. Francis of Assisi adopted a life of absolute poverty and generally revived the radical *koinonia* of the earliest church among his followers. The original band of free companions gradually hardened into more institutionalised forms but the doctrine of absolute poverty was never entirely abandoned and one result was that the friars were forbidden to own property. Difficulties arose over their houses and towards the end of the thirteenth century Pope Gregory IX, drawing on civil law, ruled that while they must renounce *dominium* of every kind, they might have *usus* or *ususfructus*. It is evident from a legal report of 1308 that the granting of property *to the use* of the 'Grey Friars' was imported to England even though the practice had no standing in common law.

It is difficult to establish to what extent the Franciscan *usus* provided the model for subsequent developments[2] but it is clear that the meteoric rise of the English 'use' commenced not long after the order entered the country. The sudden popularity of the concept was an unintended consequence of two of the sweeping legal reforms of Edward I. Seeking to prevent an increasing attrition of feudal dues, with all that implied for the royal treasury, Edward moved against 'mortmain' in 1279 and 1285 and against 'sub-infeudation' in the great statute of 1290, *Quia Emptores*.

Quia Emptores was designed to prevent the loss of landlords' economic privileges; to achieve this, tenants lost the right to create sub-tenants, although they could still sell their tenancy outright. The loss of this right had various effects; in the present context the most relevant is that it eliminated a traditional means of evading the medieval equivalent of death duty; and, given that passing on wealth to one's descendants is one of the most compulsive of human motives, it is not surprising that new ways of achieving the old results soon developed. Hence it was that transfer of land to trustworthy people, who undertook to hold it for specified purposes, became extremely popular with landowners; for the 'use' was the only way to make a bequest of land, their principal form of wealth.

The *mortmain statutes* were also intended to protect the great landlords, particularly the king himself. They sought to prevent the loss of feudal privileges suffered by landlords when one of their more pious tenants made a grant of land to the church, whether for ecclesiastical purposes or for redistribution as charitable alms-giving. The loss was permanent since the church, being a corporate personality, never died – hence the term mortmain, the *dead hand* of the church, a metaphor for impersonal ownership. The new law prohibited grants of land to the church except by royal licence. In practice, it did not diminish the flow of gifts into the 'dead hand' but it did provoke increasing recourse to the 'use' because by putting land in the hands of a trustee the expense of a royal licence could be avoided, until 1391 at least, when Richard II brought in fresh mortmain legislation to prohibit gifts 'to the use' of church bodies, without a royal licence.

By this time, however, the use was well established. Later the terms 'use' and 'trust' were used as synonyms and it was only towards the end of the sixteenth century that lawyers began to distinguish *passive uses*, which were mostly by then illegal,[3] from the *active use* or trust, which had escaped the avarice of Henry VIII. Active uses are those where the trustee, not the beneficiary, administers the property and even today most trusts are active whereas the great majority of uses had been passive. The term 'use' gradually disappeared but the trust was destined for a leading role among English legal institutions. It played an important part in the emancipation of women and is still the basis on which a wide range of bodies hold their property including, to mention but a few, the Stock Exchange, pension funds and trades unions.

THE COURT OF CONSCIENCE

The beneficiaries of 'uses' had no rights at common law and during the fourteenth century they had to rely on the conscience of the trustee or feoffee to uses as they were then known. Towards the end of the century, however, legal redress began to become available.

The common law at this time failed to deal adequately with matters such as contracts, debts and fraud as well as uses. The remedies it offered were usually confined to damages even where other relief such as enforcement of an obligation would have been appropriate. Procedural technicalities often stood in the way of a fair outcome; and even where they did not, judges or juries might be corrupted or intimidated. The king as 'the fountain of justice' had always retained a residual jurisdiction to provide justice where the courts had failed to do so. Gradually this function was delegated to the Chancellor, the head of Chancery which, with the Exchequer made up the medieval civil service. The Chancellor was the highest official of state and even today nominally ranks above the Prime Minister. But the king's chief secretary was also his chaplain, 'the keeper of the king's conscience', a high dignitary of the church. Not lawyers, but ecclesiastics trained in theology, the chancellors corrected the defects of the common law in the light of a wider view of justice.

Unlike the common-law judges the chancellors were not, at first, bound by technical rules of precedent; they had wide powers to do justice as they saw fit and exercised them with a minimum of formality. The 'court of conscience' was relatively cheap, efficient and just and its work grew rapidly. 'Equity will not suffer a wrong without a remedy' and the supervision and enforcement of uses and trusts was (and remains) a major part of equity.

IMPACT OF THE REFORMATION

The first non-ecclesiastical Chancellor was Sir Thomas More, appointed in 1529, but it was not until 1672 that the last clerical Chancellor – William, Bishop of Lincoln – ended his term of office. And Thomas More's theological convictions were sufficient to lose him his life in 1535 for his opposition to Henry VIII's break with the Roman Church. Not that More's views were particularly conventional. His famous satire *Utopia* opens with a passionate indictment of the economic and social conditions prevailing in Europe and particularly in England, contrasting this with life in Utopia which is immune to Europe's evils, thanks to its basic communism including equal rights for women, free and continuing education and equal participation in government.

Henry VIII's Reformation had different motives – dynastic and financial. He strengthened existing mortmain legislation, dissolved the monasteries and gave himself powers to confiscate other church property. Dozens of schools, colleges, 'hospitals' and so forth, were swept away in the process and although Henry and his successors refounded some of these, the overall impact was to undermine the medieval, church-centred welfare system which was, in any case, already in decline.

The gap was filled in two ways: by secular philanthropy and state intervention. Professor Jordan's classic *Philanthropy in Britain 1480-1660*[4] has chronicled how the changing attitudes that accompanied the Reformation, particularly Protestant individualism, resulted in a radical shift in the character of philanthropy. The rising middle class of urban merchants and rural gentry turned away from the church as the mechanism for giving to those in need. Instead they established innumerable secular endowments – new hospitals and almshouses, apprentice-ship schemes and workhouses, grammar schools and university colleges, loan schemes to set up young men in business, programmes of 'municipal betterment' such as building and repairing roads and bridges. For much of this they relied on the mechanism of the use or trust which consequently came to occupy a central place in the legal infrastructure of philanthropy.

But secular philanthropy was not enough and the reign of Elizabeth I saw increasing state intervention to deal with the increasing unemployment, poverty and vagrancy of the age. A statute of 1572 empowered parishes to levy a 'poor rate' to support the upkeep of almshouses and workhouses. But the problems did not go away and the Parliament of 1597 was worried by the suffering of the poor and, still more alarming, the danger of violent uprisings if nothing was done to relieve the widespread misery. The outcome was a series of statutes which shaped a lasting system of poor relief. In particular, the *Acte for the Reliefe of the Poore 1597* provided for local taxes and the appointment of overseers to set children and their parents to work, if they could not maintain themselves, to put children into apprenticeships and to provide necessary relief for the 'lame, impotent, old, blind and such other being poor and not able to work'. This often harsh system, with its distinction between the deserving and un-deserving poor, endured till the present century; it was only completely abolished in 1948, and still colours attitudes in some quarters.

The Parliament of 1597 was also conscious, however, of the potential role of private philanthropy and anxious to ensure that everything possible was done to maximise its contribution, so lessening the burden of the local poor rates. They therefore enacted *An Acte to reforme Deceiptes and Breaches of Trust, towching Landes given to charitable Uses*, observing in its preamble that charitable endowments 'have bene and are still like to be most unlawfully and uncharitably converted to the Lucre and Gayne of somme fewe greedy and covetous persons'. The *Charitable Uses Act 1597* was found to have a number of defects and it was replaced in 1601 by a better drafted and more sophisticated version, *An Acte to redresse the Misemployment of Landes Goodes and Stockes of Money heretofore given to Charitable Uses.*

THE CHARITABLE USES ACT 1601

By this time the Court of Chancery was no longer the cheap and efficient source of justice it had been in earlier times and Sir Thomas More's success in clearing a considerable backlog of cases during his brief tenure as Chancellor had not been repeated. The enforcement of *charitable* trusts encountered extra problems: the beneficiaries were often poor and the sums at issue not large enough to risk their being eaten up by the costs of litigation. Hence charitable suits in chancery were relatively rare[5] and there was a clear need for some other means of controlling dishonest or lazy trustees.

The 1601 Act gave the Lord Chancellor power to appoint commissioners to investigate 'any breach of truth, falsity, non-employment, concealment, misgovernment or conversion' of charitable funds. One of the commissioners had to be the local Bishop, a recognition perhaps of his ancient position as the 'guardian of charity'. Together with 'other persons of good and sound behaviour' he was to issue notice of the enquiry, inviting reports of breach of trust. In the subsequent hearings, witnesses were cross-examined and a jury decided whether redress was needed. If it was, the commissioners had wide powers to issue 'orders, judgements and decrees', subject only to an appeal to the Chancellor.

The 1601 Act was essentially a *remedial* statute with the aim of enforcing charitable uses. It did not aim to change the *content* of the law which had been (and continued to be) defined by the decisions of the courts in individual cases. It did, however, specify the particular 'uses' to which the commissioners' powers applied, by providing a detailed list of long-established charitable purposes. The preamble states that endowments had been given,

> Some for relief of aged, impotent and poor people, some for maintenance of sick and maimed soldiers and mariners, schools of learning, free schools and scholars in univer-

sitites; some for repair of bridges, ports, havens, causeways, churches, sea banks and highways; some for education and preferment of orphans; some for or towards the relief, stock or maintenance for houses of correction; some for marriages of poor maids; some for supportation, aid and help of young tradesmen, handicraftsmen and persons decayed; and others for relief or redemption of prisoners or captives and aid or ease of any poor inhabitants concerning payment of fifteens, setting out of soldiers and other taxes.

This remarkable catalogue of Tudor philanthropy did not, however, preclude the commissioners from enforcing trusts that were not specifically listed; it was accepted from the outset that other purposes, such as the provision of a public midwife, came within the equity of the statute provided they were for the public benefit. On the other hand, certain long-established charitable purposes *were* excluded, notably all those concerned with the advancement of religion with the exception of repairs to churches. Religion was deliberately excluded to avoid the danger that the statute might be used to alter or confiscate religious endowments should a Roman Catholic succeed to the throne.[6] This did not mean, however, that purposes such as a gift to maintain a preacher were not regarded as charitable; they were, but they fell outside the remit of the commissioners and those who sought their enforcement had to apply direct to the Court of Chancery.

In short, the 1601 Act did not (and was not intended to) provide a comprehensive definition of charity. Nevertheless, its preamble exercised a profound effect on the later development of the legal meaning of charity. In the hands of progressive judges, a liberal construction of the preamble has allowed the meaning of charity to evolve in response to changing social needs by admitting innovatory purposes on the basis of analogies with those listed in the 1601 Act, not to mention analogies with such analogies and so on. From time to time, however, more conservative judges have blocked such development by insisting on a restrictive interpretation, or on analogies with restrictive interpretations.

But since the courts have always admitted the advancement of religion as a valid charitable purpose, despite the 1601 Act, it is difficult to see why the preamble should be given any special status whatsoever. In practice, if not in theory, the courts have come round to this view[7] and it is submitted that the real basis of the legal meaning of charity is accumulated case law, not the 1601 statute.[8]

THE AGE OF REASON

The early Charity Commissioners were a great success at first, uncovering and setting to rights a great many misuses of charitable funds throughout the Stuart period. After the Glorious Revolution of 1688 attitudes changed rapidly, however, and the practice of appointing commissioners quickly fell into disuse.

The eighteenth century, the 'age of reason', was also, for many, an age of the most abject poverty and misery imaginable. Conditions were worst in rural areas where the enclosures brought widespread destitution, but little better in the towns with their overcrowding, disease, exploitation of child labour, intolerably long working hours, low pay and inhuman working conditions. Indifference to the fate of the poor was widespread and the Established Church was no exception: 'The poor', remarked a Bishop in the House of Lords, 'have nothing to do with the laws but to obey them'.[9]

It is not surprising, therefore, to find that eighteenth-century judges were often markedly hostile to charity, tending wherever possible to defend the interests of the heir at the expense of charitable bequests.[10] Their hostility was shared by Parliament, as the debates preceding the enactment of the *Mortmain Act 1736* make clear, e.g.:

> I cannot but think that a man's heirs-at-law have some sort of natural right to succeed after his death, at least to his land estate. . . . The giving of any such charity I shall always look upon rather as an act of injustice towards the heir-at-law, than as an act of charity in the donor. . . . To assist the widow and fatherless, to nourish the tender infant, and succour the helpless old; in short, to relieve the poor distressed, who cannot provide for themselves, is a duty incumbent upon every society . . . but, my Lords, this duty is to be discharged with great caution . . . for if by giving what we call charity we encourage laziness, idleness, and extravagance . . . the action is so far from being pious, charitable, or commendable, that it becomes impious, ridiculous and injurious, to our native country. . . . The funds for relief of deserving poor are sufficient.[11]

The Mortmain Act invalidated charitable gifts of land or buildings unless made at least a year before the donor's death. It provoked a great deal of litigation with somewhat mixed results. In the short term it primarily benefited heirs who would otherwise have been disinherited. But paradoxically, its more lasting effect was a considerable *widening* of the legal meaning of charity. This was because bequests for non-charitable purposes were not caught by the Mortmain Act with the result that, in their anxiety to help the disinherited, successive judges held a variety of purposes charitable which had not been so in earlier times – museums and botanical gardens, for example, and trusts to prevent cruelty to animals.

In the case of bequests other than land and buildings, which were not caught by the Mortmain legislation, the judges took an entirely different and often inconsistent line: from one day to the next charity would become a very narrow concept in order that heirs should not lose out.[12] Such cases bequeathed a category of contradictory precedents, although fortunately they were relatively few in number.

THE VICTORIANS

Towards the end of the eighteenth century a new spirit of concern for the downtrodden masses began to emerge. Many of the leading reformers experienced some sort of sudden conversion to their vocation:

> Shaftesbury, at the age of fourteen, saw a pauper funeral and vowed to dedicate his life to the uplift of the downtrodden and oppressed; Barnardo, destined for the foreign mission field, was turned to work for London's waifs by the cry of a homeless child – 'I don't live nowhere'. . . . Octavia Hill left art and teaching for housing at the revelation of conditions in Marylebone. . . . These examples could be multiplied almost indefinitely.[13]

The new spirit of concern took two forms: service and pressure for reform. The origins of the Welfare State in the service-providing charities created by Victorian social concern is well known and does not need recounting here. As regards the development of the concept of charity, however, it is important to note that the Victorians increasingly abandoned the traditional endowed trust format for the more democratic voluntary association or society, a development which had already begun in the eighteenth century but was greatly quickened by the new emphasis on providing welfare services. Such bodies did not, however, escape the law of charity, because ever since 1610[14] the courts had held that an 'implied' trust underlay their activities so that they were governed by the same rules and regulations as 'express' trusts.

Pressure for reform was an equally important element in nineteenth-century social concern, however, as many recognised that charitable service-giving would have only a superficial impact if the underlying causes of social misery remained untouched. Beginning with the anti-slavery campaign, the reformers tirelessly pressed for legislation to end the exploitation of child labour and improve conditions in factories, to humanise the appallingly harsh criminal law and end the squalor of the prisons, and to remedy a host of other social evils.

These two aspects of the Victorian social conscience are often treated as separate, even conflicting, phenomena. But this is a distortion – in reality there was considerable overlap, with many people, such as Lord Shaftesbury, playing an important role in both developments. The picture is not unmixed – like many an individual, the service-giving charities not infrequently acquired reactionary attitudes in their later years – but service and pressure for reform were often closely linked.

THE REFORM OF CHARITY LAW

Needless to say, the law of charity did not escape the reformers' attentions. The hostility of the eighteenth-century Chancery Court had virtually abolished control over charitable endowments: 'many trusts had fallen into the hands of corrupt or lazy trustees; or had disappeared; or were being misapplied; others had become hopelessly out of date.'[15] And when public concern did revive, the Court of Chancery offered little hope of dealing with the problems: its inefficiency and crippling costs in the early nineteenth century were notorious, as Dickens' *Bleak House* records. A new approach was needed.

In 1818 a Royal Commission was established under the chairmanship of Lord Brougham, a passionate advocate of reform. The Brougham commissioners were given powers to investigate and enquire into the administration of charities. Their reports vindicated Brougham's diagnosis, uncovering widespread abuses, but could not overcome the deficiencies of Chancery. Eventually, in 1835, a Parliamentary Select Committee recommended the establishment of an 'independent authority' to supervise charitable endowments. The proposal encountered considerable opposition and it was eighteen years before the *Charitable Trusts Act 1853* finally reached the statute book.

The 1853 Act established a permanent Charity Commission which improved matters to some extent, but the Commissioners' powers were relatively limited, particularly with respect to modernising out-of-date trusts where they were restricted by the strict application of the *cy-près* doctrine. This dictated that where it became impossible for trustees to carry out the terms of a charitable trust, the court had power to direct that the endowment should be applied to some other purpose as near as possible (*cy-près*) to the original one, even where all agreed that some other, cy-not-so-près, purpose would be more useful.

The reformers favoured considerable relaxation of the *cy-près* doctrine but they failed to achieve any comprehensive measure of this kind, although the *Endowed Schools Act 1869* provided wide powers to modify the purposes of *educational* charities and the *City of London Parochial Charities Act 1883* gave the Charity Commissioners a free hand to modernise the archaic endowments of that city.

The effects of these reforms were enhanced by extensive changes to the Court of Chancery. Between 1830 and 1858 there were no fewer than ten separate Acts aimed at piecemeal reform of the glaring inadequacies of Chancery and in 1873 it was merged with the common-law jurisdiction, becoming the Chancery Division of the High Court.

CHARITY AND EQUITY TODAY

Like its predecessor of 1601, the *Charitable Trusts Act 1853* was a remedial statute, not concerned with the content of the law, which remained the province of case by case decisions. The last of the great remedial statutes was the *Charities Act 1960*. This implemented many of the recommendations of the Nathan Committee which had reported eight years earlier.[15] The act consolidated much previous legislation (it repealed over thirty separate earlier statutes which were obsolete or superseded), strengthened the powers of the Charity Commissioners and extended them to unendowed charities, and swept away the last vestiges of the mortmain legislation. It also provided for the introduction of a register (and the compulsory registration) of charities.

Today the system of equity governing the behaviour and privileges of charities is composed of three elements. The courts are the ultimate authority, principally the Chancery Division of the High Court; from its decisions appeal may be made to the Court of Appeal and from there (or, in some cases, directly) to the House of Lords. The second element in the system is the Charity Commissioners with their staff of over 300 lawyers and civil servants. They exercise a mixture of administrative and quasi-judicial functions and are, in effect, an extension of the High Court.

The third element in the system is the Inland Revenue; its Charities Division, located in Bootle, has about 150 staff. The Revenue plays an important role because it administers the majority of the tax concessions enjoyed by charities. Before 1960, it was the main arbiter of charitable status but that function now lies with the Charity Commissioners. The Revenue is still free, however, to rule that charities are not entitled to concessions because their income has not been applied to charitable purposes and it consequently has an important regulatory role. The complementary roles of the Inland Revenue and the Charity Commissioners are discussed in greater detail in chapter 8.

Both Scotland and Northern Ireland have somewhat different approaches. In Northern Ireland, the law is closely modelled on the system obtaining in England and Wales but the administrative mechanisms are different. Scottish law takes a different approach altogether, although as regards taxation Scotland is treated as if it were part of England and Wales, which causes some resentment. Appendix 1 provides a more detailed sketch of charity law and its administration in Scotland and Northern Ireland.

Close cousins to the English law of charity are found in many Commonwealth countries and also in the USA. The legal meaning of charity has diverged to some extent in the various jurisdictions but there are still close similarities; American and Australian precedents are still admissible in English courts, and *vice versa*. And, as will be seen, the divergences often provide interesting food for thought.

4. The Legal Meaning of Charity

I do not think that the word 'charity' has ever been defined or is capable of exact definition. Judges of great authority have said that it has a technical meaning peculiar to the law, that it is wide and elastic and that it has a much wider meaning in law than it has in popular speech, but they seem always to go on immediately to the meaning of 'charitable purposes' which is really the technical term involved . . . This may be only a matter of words but it is better, to avoid confusion of thought, to keep to the phrase 'charitable purposes' than to confuse it with the transcendental idea of charity which, perhaps, can only be embodied in a figure in a stained glass window.

(Chief Chancery Master R. E. Ball)[1]

No English statute has ever attempted to give a fundamental definition of the legal meaning of charity. The preamble to the 1601 statute provides a list of charitable purposes but no formal definition; and, as already mentioned, the courts have always treated the list as not exhaustive but illustrative. The 1960 Act states that '"charity" means any institution, corporate or not, which is established for charitable purpose'[2] but when one turns to its subsequent 'definitions' one finds that '"Charitable purposes" means purposes exclusively charitable according to the law of England and Wales'.[3] The law referred to is accumulated case law so that the legal meaning of charity is, in effect, only systematically defined by (literally) thousands of precedents, laid down over the centuries by the decisions of generations of judges.

The starting point for this long process of evolution was not, of course, the concept of charity current in present-day ordinary language – not, that is, hand-outs for those in need – but the much wider theological notion, *agape*, discussed in chapter 2, and there defined as 'equal and unconditional concerns for the welfare of every fellow human being'. Since this conception was central to Christian belief and religious teaching, the early judges had no need of formal definitions.

In its theological sense, charity is not concerned only with the relief of poverty; hence the enduring place of such purposes as education in the legal understanding of the term. Nevertheless, theology has always seen help for the disadvantaged and downtrodden as the quintessence of practical charity and the prior claim of poverty was generally accepted in legal thinking under the Tudors and Stuarts. In the eighteenth century, however, the distorting effect of the *Mortmain Act 1736* weakened this emphasis; and the influence of theology on judicial thinking gradually waned so that the legal meaning of charity came to rest on established precedent.

The eighteenth-century judges recognised that the 1601 preamble did not provide an adequate definition of charity.[4] For them the concept of 'public benefit' became the key to the legal meaning of the term; so in 1767, for example, the Chancellor, Lord Camden, defined a charitable gift as 'A gift to a general public use which extends to the poor as well as the rich'.[5] More generally, the preamble was seen not as 'the exclusive touchstone of legal charity' but as 'a valuable and historical catalogue of charitable uses'.[6] The purposes it listed were accepted without question but this did not mean that those it excluded were not charitable, provided they were 'for the public benefit'.

Hence in the crucial case of *Morice v. Bishop of Durham*,[7] counsel for the Bishop could argue, correctly but unsuccessfully, that 'Upon the authorities almost everything, from which the public derive benefit, may be considered a charity'.[8] This crucial case of 1805 hinged on a bequest for 'such objects of benevolence and liberality as the Bishop of Durham, in his own discretion, should most approve of'. Was this a charitable trust (if it were the heirs would lose out since, because the gift did not involve land or buildings, it would elude the Mortmain Act)? The judge held that it was not:

> Do purposes of liberality and benevolence mean the same as objects of charity? That word, in its widest sense, denotes all the good affections men ought to bear towards each other; in its most restricted and common sense, relief of the poor. In neither of these senses is it employed in this Court. Here its signification is derived chiefly from the Statute of *Elizabeth*. Those purposes are considered charitable, which that statute enumerates, or which by analogies are deemed within its spirit and intendment. . . . But it is clear liberality and benevolence can find numberless objects, not included in that statute in the largest construction of it.[9]

From this time on the preamble gained an authority it had never had before and which, it is submitted, is poor history and, inasmuch as it is irreconcilable with the full range of accepted precedents, worse logic.

Fortunately this has been recognised by the courts, as a recent authoritative statement shows. Referring to the requirement that to qualify as charitable a purpose must fall 'within the spirit and intendment' of the 1601 preamble, Lord Wilberforce pointed out that this

> ... does not mean quite what it says: for it is now accepted that what must be regarded is not the wording of the preamble itself, but the effect of decisions given by the courts as to its scope, decisions which have endeavoured to keep the law as to charities moving according as new social needs arise or old ones become obsolete or satisfied.[10]

CLASSIFICATIONS

Morice v. Bishop of Durham is, however, deservedly famous for a different reason; while putting the case for the next of kin, Sir Samuel Romilly formulated a classification of charitable purposes which is still influential today:

> There are four objects within one of which all charity, to be administered in this court, must fall. First, relief of the indigent; in various ways: money: provisions: education: medical assistance; etc; Secondly, the advancement of learning; Thirdly the advancement of religion; and Fourthly, which is the most difficult, the advancement of objects of general public utility.[11]

In 1891, nearly a century later, Lord Macnaghten adapted Romilly's classification and gave it the seal of judicial approval:

> How far then, it may be asked, does the popular meaning of the word 'charity' correspond with its legal meaning? 'Charity' in the legal sense comprises four principal divisions: trusts for the relief of poverty; trusts for the advancement of education; trusts for the advancement of religion; and trusts for other purposes beneficial to the community not falling under any of the preceding heads.[12]

The phrasing of the fourth head – 'other purposes beneficial to the community' – does not, however, mean *all* other such purposes but only those established by precedent – i.e. *some* other purposes beneficial to the community.

The Romilly/MacNaghten classification is followed by most textbooks and other guides to the field although often with some criticism of its adequacy. But there is a growing tendency to expand the classification, accepting the first three heads of the Romilly/MacNaghten scheme:

1. *relief of poverty*
2. *advancement of education* (including research and the arts)
3. *advancement of religion*

but sub-dividing the fourth, 'other purposes' head as covering too large a multitude of charitable purposes. There are at least four other major categories which might be described as:

4. *promotion of health* (including relief of aged and disabled people)
5. *social rehabilitation* (including help for refugees and disaster victims; ex-prisoners and other ex-offenders; alcoholics and drug addicts)
6. *provision and maintenance of public amenities* (including roads, bridges etc; libraries, museums etc; parks, recreational facilities etc; preservation of historic monuments; etc.)
7. *protection of animals and the natural environment generally*

as well as a number of other, miscellaneous purposes making up a residual category of

8. *other purposes 'beneficial to the community'* (including the promotion of agriculture, industry and commerce; the protection of human life and property; the preservation of public order; and the defence of the realm).

CRITERIA

To be a charity in law, a trust or organisation must have, as its primary aims and objectives, the achievement of one or more of the purposes just classified. And it must have no primary purposes which fall outside those which the courts, over the centuries, have deemed charitable: the law requires a charity's purposes to be *exclusively* charitable. But having exclusively 'approved' purposes, though necessary, is not a sufficient condition for recognition as a charity. The courts use wider criteria, summed up in the phrase 'public benefit', to decide on charitable status.

'Public benefit' implies, in fact, a two-pronged test: is there a *benefit* and is it a *public* benefit? The question of benefit is partly a matter of whether purposes fall within one of the categories recognised as charitable by the courts. But that, by itself, is not enough: the benefit must be real. So, for instance, on hearing that an artist's studio and its contents, bequeathed as a public museum, contained nothing of aesthetic merit, Lord Harman disallowed the gift, observing:

> I can conceive of no useful object to be served in foisting on the public this mass of junk. It has neither public utility nor educative value.[13]

Even a genuine benefit is insufficient if it is not also a *public* benefit. A trust for the education of one's grandchildren would fall squarely within the approved territory; but it would not be charitable because the class of beneficiaries would be too narrow. A charity must be 'beneficial to the whole of the community or to a sufficiently important section of the community'.[14] But what is a *sufficiently important* section of the community? The courts have never yet provided any very precise or comprehensive answer so that the nature of the boundary between public and private benefit remains obscure, not to say perplexing. This issue is examined more fully in the next chapter.

It is clear, however, that the requirement that all benefit be public rules out any profit distribution.[15] A commercial company may confer considerable benefits of a charitable type on the community but it cannot be a charity. This does not mean, however, that charities cannot charge for their services even if the charges yield a profit; but the profit must be applied to the charities' purposes. Charities must be non-profit-distributing organisations.

Similarly, mutual benefit (self-help) societies cannot generally be charities, if their income derives in the main from members' subscriptions etc. and their benefits accrue entirely or primarily to those same members. An exception is made where benefits go only to members who become impoverished or where non-members can benefit substantially or if the funds are not primarily derived from members' subscriptions. But the general principle rules out most friendly societies and other insurance schemes, trades unions and professional associations, and the majority of clubs. Charity, in the legal sense, requires an element of altruism.

Finally, *political activity*. Since 1917, the courts have held that no 'political' objective, such as seeking a change in the law, can be a charitable purpose. That does not mean that charities cannot engage in political activity in pursuit of a valid, non-political purpose; but it must be a *means* to an end not an end in itself. Chapter 7 provides a more detailed analysis of this issue.

To sum up: a charitable purpose, in the legal sense, is one which yields an identifiable benefit to the community (or a 'sufficiently important section' of it); and this, the courts have held, rules out profit distribution, self-help and political objectives. In short, the legal meaning of charity may be summed up in the words, the advancement of purposes beneficial to the community: the promotion of 'public benefit'.

FLEXIBILITY

Given the courts' preference for relying on tests (criteria) rather than definitions, what qualifies as legally charitable gradually changes and evolves. There is undoubtedly an attractive aspect to this, as Lord Sachs has pointed out:

> The wider test – advancement of purposes beneficial to the community or objects of general public utility – has an admirable breadth and flexibility which enables it to be reasonably applied from generation to generation to meet changing circumstances: it has such patent advantages that for my part I appreciate the wisdom of the legislature in refraining from providing a detailed definition of charitable purposes in the Act of 1960. . . . There is much to be said for flexibility in such matters.[16]

Certainly anyone who examines the myriad variety of cases that have come before the courts will recognise that more tightly defined criteria might not easily accommodate the endless inventiveness of those who create charitable trusts and organisations. But there is another aspect to judicial discretion which is less universally popular. The most striking example of this is the Court of Appeal's essentially unprecedented decision, in 1917, that political purposes could not be charitable.[17] More generally, what a court sees as a test 'reasonably applied . . . to meet changing circumstances', will not necessarily coincide with what those working in the charitable field see as reasonable, or with public opinion generally.

... OR THE DEAD HAND OF PRECEDENT?

In any case, the flexibility of the case-law approach is not unlimited. It is governed by the doctrine of precedent – *stare decisis*: 'stay with the decided cases' – and no judge will lightly ignore previous rulings on cases where the facts closely resemble those before the court. Consequently judges may find themselves saddled with precedents which they consider inappropriate but feel compelled to follow.

High Court judges are not, in fact, obliged to follow the decisions of their colleagues and predecessors but refusal to do so is rare; they are more likely to evade the precedent by distinguishing between the facts of the two cases, a gambit which at times results in somewhat tortuous logic. High Court judges must follow precedents laid down by superior courts. The Court of Appeal not infrequently overrules High Court precedents but, with few exceptions, does not depart from its own. Decisions of the House of Lords are binding on all lower courts. The Law Lords may, however, depart from any previous decisions although in practice they have rarely overturned their own precedents and seem unlikely to do so except where there has been a radical change of circumstances.

In short, there is no precedent which cannot be challenged. But such challenges are fairly rare, for as Professor Glanville Williams observes:

> Lawyers are much too prone to assume that what has been decided cannot be upset. It often happens that a plainly wrong decision is given at first instance or even by the Court of Appeal, which is followed unquestioningly for many years because counsel do not advise their clients to take the point further on appeal. When eventually, some counsel is found who has the courage and acumen to take the point, the precedent is reversed. Now that the House of Lords has decided that it can question its own previous decisions, there is hardly any decided point that cannot be reopened if the arguments against it are strong enough.[18]

But while this is true in principle, it is difficult to put into practice in the case of charity law as the cost of such an action is so great that few existing or would-be charities are prepared to gamble the necessary time and money against such an uncertain return. Most would prefer any changes they see as desirable to be brought about by legislation. The *Recreational Charities Act 1958* provides a model for this approach. It did not seek to change the basis of the law; instead it supplemented case law with guidelines in the specific area of recreation. If – a big if – parliamentary time could be found, amending legislation of this kind is probably the simplest way of modernising the law where well-established precedents obstruct adaptation to changing circumstances.

THE IMPORTANCE OF BEING CHARITABLE

The courts' long and continuing struggle to give a coherent and consistent meaning to the terms 'charity' and 'charitable' would not, of course, excite a great deal of interest if the legal meaning of charity were merely a question of semantics. But it is much more than that: charitable status confers a number of significant privileges.

Tax concessions are, perhaps, the most obvious of these. Provided that the funds are applied to charitable purposes, charities are exempted from income tax and corporation tax and from Capital Transfer, Capital Gains and Development Land Tax. They are entitled to a 50 per cent reduction in local rates (100 per cent in Northern Ireland) and do not have to pay Stamp Duty or the Employer's National Insurance surcharge. Equally important are gifts and bequests to charities since donors can avoid income tax, corporation tax, Capital Gains and Capital Transfer Tax on the sums they give for charitable purposes. The total benefit to charities is well in excess of £200 million per annum and given that there are fewer than 150,000 legal charities, the average annual benefit must run to several thousand pounds.

The *legal* benefits of charitable status are less important than they used to be. Formerly unless a trust was charitable it had to have clearly identified beneficiaries; 'purpose trusts' – i.e. those defined in terms of purposes rather than beneficiaries – were, with few exceptions, not allowed. Voluntary organisations which were refused charitable status consequently encountered many difficulties. In recent years, the courts have taken a considerably more liberal line but there are still some residual problems and many feel that validation of all purpose trusts is long overdue.[19]

Finally, charitable status is extremely important for fundraising. A 'registered charity' is more likely to inspire the confidence of potential donors among the general public. More importantly, many voluntary organisations derive a substantial slice of their income from charitable foundations. But to do so is difficult unless a body is a registered charity; a fair proportion of foundations are bound by their constitutions to give only to charities. Charitable foundations are not, in fact, obliged by law to give only to charities but they cannot make grants for non-charitable purposes. Grants to bodies which are not charities come under close scrutiny by the Inland Revenue and many foundations have reluctantly concluded that the time and cost of making such grants cannot easily be justified.

In short, charitable status is a passport to important financial advantages. The next three chapters analyse more closely some of the rules which govern access to the privileged ranks of charity and chapter 8 examines the role of the chief gate-keepers: the Charity Commissioners and the Inland Revenue.

II. The Frontiers of Charity

5. Who Shall Benefit?

I am quite aware that a trust may be charitable, and yet not confined to the poor; but I doubt very much whether a trust would be declared to be charitable which excluded the poor.

(Lord Justice Lindley)[1]

Beauty, wit . . .
Love, friendship, charity, are subjects all
To envious and calumniating time.[2]

'Public benefit' is the chief criterion used by the courts in awarding charitable status. To qualify as charitable, trusts of every type must meet the overriding requirement of being 'beneficial to the public at large or a sufficiently important section of the public'.[3] But what exactly is a *public* benefit? who are 'the public'? and what is a 'sufficiently important section' of it?

The courts have never attempted any systematic definitions, at least in the charitable field, but lexicographers rush in where lawyers fear to tread:

> **Public** . . . 1. Of or pertaining to the people as a whole; common, national, popular, late ME. 2. Done or made by or on behalf of the community as a whole . . . 3. That is open to, may be used by, or may or must be shared by, all members of the community; generally accessible or available. . . .[4]

One might expect, then, that a *public* benefit would be one shared by all members of the community, an expectation reinforced by the traditional insistence that the practical expression of charity in its theological sense, is *koinonia*: 'sharing' (see chapter 2). It is only fair to say that the courts' thinking remains heavily influenced by such conceptions; nevertheless, not everyone will find it easy to understand in what sense the benefits of charities such as Eton or expensive private clinics are 'generally accessible or available to the community as a whole'. The Oxford lexicographers provide a clue, however, to the historical roots of this state of affairs:

> **Public school.** 1580. A school which is public. 1. In England, orig., A grammar-school, endowed for the use or benefit of the public.... In modern use, applied esp. to such of these as have developed into large boarding-schools, drawing (their pupils) from well-to-do classes. . . . 2. In Scotland, British (ex-)colonies, and US: A school provided at the public expense. . . . as part of a system of public (and usu. free) education.[5]

Despite the changes to which this alludes, public schools (and various other bodies 'drawing from the well-to-do classes') have retained their charitable status. Consequently, like 'charity' and 'charitable', the term 'public' has acquired a specialised, technical meaning in law, somewhat removed from everyday language.

CHARITY AND POVERTY

This was not always so. The statute of 1601 was an integral part of the wider poor-law legislation and it is clear beyond a doubt that one of its chief purposes was to ensure that trusts which conferred no benefit on the poor could be compelled to do so. Reliable evidence for this is the lengthy commentary, written shortly after the Act was passed, by the barrister and Member of Parliament, Sir Francis Moore, who was probably a member of the committee that drafted the legislation enacted in 1601. Moore enjoyed a high reputation as a Chancery lawyer and his *Reading* on the 1601 Act has always been considered authoritative.

Professor Chesterman's useful review[6] draws attention to this document's almost obsessive concern with poverty. Moore insists that 'Poverty is the principal and *essential* circumstance to bring the gift within the compass of this statute'[7] and that while a number of the purposes listed by the preamble do not explicitly refer to poverty – Moore specifically mentions the aged, the sick and the maintenance of schools of learning – the intention of the statute was to exclude benefit for those who could afford to pay.[8]

He recognises that in some cases, such as the repair of a public bridge, the poor cannot be helped without benefiting the better-off as well:

> But it can be objected that . . . where the use expressed in the case is to all the inhabitants, which include rich as well as poor, accordingly the use in the case does not match the use in the statute, to which argument I reply: that if . . . the poor cannot be relieved without also benefiting the rich, the rich also in this unseverable case will benefit by being counted with the poor. . . . Also, the commissioners in their decree can order the employment solely to the poor if they think fit, without any violation, and thereby rectify the intent of . . . the statute.[9]

But as Gareth Jones has pointed out, Moore 'was careful to distinguish a trust which incidentally benefited the rich from one whose sole object was to benefit them. . . . So a trust to erect a mill on private ground where the poor cannot grind their corn free, was not within the statute.'[10]

During the eighteenth century this latter point was never entirely lost; in 1767 the Lord Chancellor could declare:

> Definition of charity: a gift to a general public use which extends to the poor as well as the rich.[11]

But the wider intention of the 1601 statute – that wherever possible charitable benefits should not go to those who could afford to pay – gradually fell from favour. Hence by 1827, the senior judge in Chancery, Leach V.C., could rule charitable a trust to establish a school for educating the sons of gentlemen; ignoring a precedent of 1700 which had established that only free schools came within the ambit of the 1601 Act,[12] he held that

> The institution of a school for the sons of gentlemen is not, in popular language, a charity; but in the view of the statute of Elizabeth, all schools are so to be considered.[13]

At the time such a decision had few implications for public policy, as in 1827 charities enjoyed only legal privileges. During the Napoleonic wars, however, when a temporary income tax had been introduced between 1799 and 1816, there had been an express exemption for 'any corporation, fraternity or society of persons established for charitable purposes only'. This privileged position was renewed when income tax was reintroduced in 1842; and 'schools for the sons of gentlemen' – which had become charitable in the intervening period – were not excepted. This did not pass unchallenged: in 1863 the Chancellor of the Exchequer, W. E. Gladstone, introduced a Bill to abolish all charities' exempt status on the grounds that 'it represented an undiscriminating public subsidy for a large group of organisations which were not subject to any adequate form of public scrutiny', singling out, among other 'undeserving' cases, 'élite schools . . . which had little or nothing to do with educating the poor'.[14]

Although the Bill failed to muster a majority, Gladstone's crusade was not without effect. Before 1863 the tax commissioners had exempted all charities; thereafter they took a view more in accord with the spirit of the 1601 Act. For the purposes of tax exemption, 'charitable' was newly interpreted as implying a significant element of relief for the poor and it was not until the *Pemsel* case nearly forty years later that this interpretation was overturned. In *Pemsel*[15] a majority of four to two in the House of Lords held that in connection with tax exemptions, the term 'charitable' bore the same broad meaning it had acquired in general case law. Their Lordships did not greatly concern themselves with whether their decision would detract from a sensible public policy as the task before them (as they saw it) was merely to determine the correct interpretation of the *Income Tax Act 1842*. 'With the policy of taxing charities I have nothing to do', Lord MacNaghten correctly observed,[16] but the *consequences* for public policy were nevertheless very considerable.

PUBLIC BENEFIT TODAY

The drift away from the original 'spirit and intendment' of the 1601 Act continues. In 1922 the precedents were still held clearly to indicate that there must be an element of poverty if a gift for aged persons was to be upheld;[17] but in 1950 Dankwerts, J. took the view that the words 'aged, impotent and poor' in the 1601 preamble were to be read disjunctively so that aged sick and disabled people need not also be poor to be legitimate objects of charity.[18] This flies in the face of all the historical evidence but it has been generally followed in subsequent decisions by the courts.

Some boundaries are recognised, however; it is generally accepted that gifts for the *exclusive* benefit of the rich are not charitable.[19] It is reassuring to learn that a trust to establish a rest-home for 'impotent' millionaires would fail[20] although this observation does prompt the suspicion that present-day courts might hold that no one less wealthy than a millionaire counts as rich.

More generally, it is now well established that the standard of public benefit required by the courts – 'a sufficiently important section of the public' – varies from charity to charity. Observing that the law of charity had been built up not logically but empirically, Lord Simonds observed:

> It would not, therefore, be surprising to find that, while in every category of legal charity some element of public benefit must be present, the court had adopted the same measure in regard to different categories, but had accepted one standard in regard to those gifts which are alleged to be for the advancement of education and another for those which are alleged to be for the advancement of religion, and it may be yet another in regard to the relief of poverty.[21]

Where a gift appears to be for the relief of poverty or the advancement of education or of religion, the courts will normally assume it to be for the benefit of the community unless evidence to the contrary is produced.[22] But other gifts will encounter a sterner scrutiny and a stiffer standard. *Tudor on Charities* takes the view that in such cases, as a general rule,

> The requirement of benefit to the community will not be satisfied if any person physically capable of and desirous of enjoying the benefits of the trust is . . . excluded from these benefits because he is not engaged in a particular trade, business or calling or because he is not the adherent of a particular religion or political party.[23]

But this should not be taken as excluding *minority interests*: a trust for a botanical garden, for example, is valid because, as Lord Simonds has pointed out, there is a distinction.

> between a form of relief extended to the whole community yet, by its very nature, advantageous only to a few, and a form of relief accorded to a selected few out of a larger number equally willing and able to take advantage of it.[24]

And it is important to remember that the public benefit

requirement does not mean that everyone in the relevant section of the public must derive some benefit from a trust; merely that they must be *eligible* for benefit. An endowment to provide housing for the elderly, for example, may only benefit one, not necessarily poor, aged person at any particular time.

Nevertheless, the doctrine still stands that no trust can be charitable that excludes the poor,[25] at least in principle. But what about in practice? Two cases will be examined – public schools and private hospitals. Do they serve a 'sufficiently important section of the community' to qualify for today's generous tax concessions?

THE EVOLUTION OF THE PUBLIC SCHOOLS

At the time of the 1601 Act, no educated person would have disagreed that education was a form of charity. Sir Thomas Browne, some thirty years later, was in no doubt about the wide character of charity:

> I hold not so narrow a conceit of this vertue, as to conceive that to give almes, is onely to be Charitable ... as many wayes as we may doe good, so many wayes we may bee Charitable; there are infirmities, not onely of body, but of soule, and fortunes, which doe require the mercifull hand of our abilities. I cannot contemn a man for ignorance. ... It is no greater Charity to cloath his body, then apparell the nakednesse of his Soule. ... It is the cheapest way of beneficence, and like the naturall charity of the Sunne illuminates another without obscuring it selfe. To be reserved and caitif in this part of goodnesse, is the sordidest piece of covetousnesse, and more contemptible than the pecuniary avarice. ... I make not therefore my head a grave, but a treasure of knowledge; I intend no Monopoly, but a Community in learning; I study not for my owne sake onely, but for theirs that study not for themselves. I envy no man that knowes more than my selfe, but pity them that know lesse. ... I cannot fall out or contemne a man for an errour, or conceive why a difference in opinion should divide an affection: for controversies, disputes, and argumentations ... doe not infringe the Lawes of Charity.[26]

But not all education was charitable at law; under the Stuarts, as discussed earlier, a charitable trust was not just any gift for charity but only those which benefited the poor or, where unavoidable, the rich as well as the poor. And even today, if the court is of the opinion that the purpose of the gift or trust is not to benefit the public at large (or a sufficiently large and defined section of the public) but for the benefit of particular individuals, it will not in law be a charitable purpose even though the benefit taken by those individuals is of the very character stated in the 1601 preamble.[27]

Until the Reformation the great majority of English schools were church-run, mostly attached to the great cathedrals, monasteries and universities. Hundreds of these were swept away after Henry VIII's break with Rome and his subsequent confiscation of church property; by no means all were refounded and English education took years to recover. In the early days great importance was attached to educating the children of the poor: the 1382 charter of Winchester College, for example, had as its main object 'free education in Latin for the sons of poor people' and, in 1440, Eton College was to be 'a school for boys of good character and decent life, poor and needy'. This emphasis continued under the Tudors and Stuarts and similar good intentions are to be found in the original deeds of schools such as Dulwich and Highgate. Fees were expressly ruled out in some cases, Westminster School, for instance, and Sevenoaks:

> A grammar school in some convenient house in Sennoke, to teach and instruct poor children taking nothing of them or their parents or friends for the teaching, to be called the Free Grammar School of Queen Elizabeth.

The title 'Free Grammar School' did not, however, necessarily mean that fees were not charged – 'free' meant free from control by the church – and fee-paying has a long history. In 1414, Durham school was reconstituted

> To instruct all willing to learn or study . . . the poor indeed freely for the love of God, if they or their parents humbly ask for it, but taking from those who by themselves or their friends are willing to pay the moderate fees accustomed to be paid in other schools of grammar.[28]

Eton's original statute allowed for twenty fee-payers but even by Elizabethan times the college's fee-payers outnumbered those taken free.

By the nineteenth century, many of the schools bore little resemblance to the intentions of their founders. Harrow, for instance, had been established to provide free education for local scholars but by 1816 there were only three free scholars among several hundred fee-payers. Occasional challenges in the courts were largely unsuccessful[29] and many endowments were diverted to the private use of headmasters and others.

In 1860, the warden and fellows at Winchester still gobbled up half the college revenues – eight times what was spent on the staff; the press took up the issue and misappropriation of school endowments became a public scandal.[30] The findings of the Clarendon Commission – set up the following year to investigate the leading schools – not only led to their extensive reform but also prompted the establishment of the Taunton Commission in 1864 to examine the host of lesser establishments. The Commission took its task seriously and laboured long and hard, uncovering innumerable abuses. In 1867 they presented their report:

> Though often individually quite small, in total the sum of endowment money was colossal. If all these endowments were put together and redistributed on a national scale, they could form the financial core of a great new national system of secondary education. The Commission drew up detailed plans for this: the control to be central, via Parliament, a national exam system, regular inspection, a modern curriculum including science. But more than this, the system was to be for everyone, from every class: those too poor to pay would be educated free, those who could afford to pay would do so, augmenting the merged endowments.[31]

A bill containing these radical proposals was put to Parliament but emasculated by frenzied behind-the-scenes lobbying and the eventual *Endowed Schools Act 1869* was a much tamer affair. But although the vision of a classless, national education system faded, at least for the time being, the Act nevertheless conferred sweeping powers on the new Endowed Schools Commissioners. The *cy-près* doctrine was pushed aside – new governing instruments, which completely ignored the founders' intentions, could be imposed on ancient endowments.* The Commissioners

---

*The Labour Party seems never to have realised that the *Endowed Schools Act 1869* enabled Secretaries of State for Education to impose their will on virtually all public schools. At any rate, in 1973 a Conservative government carried off a poker-faced repeal of the Act without a murmur of protest from the opposite benches.

could have ensured that the poor were not excluded from any public school; but as it turned out they had the opposite effect. School after school was allowed to abandon any remaining pretence of catering for the poor or even of providing more than a handful of free places.

By this time fees had been introduced even at schools such as Manchester Grammar and Nottingham High where the founders had expressly forbidden them. A parallel development was the creation of many new schools which from the start were intended only for fee-payers. The overall result was that public schools ceased to be 'public' in the normal sense of 'on behalf of the community as a whole'.

PRIVATE EDUCATION IN THE 1980s

Today only 6 per cent of children at school – about half a million – are educated outside the state system. But only about a quarter of these are at public schools or their junior counterparts, preparatory schools. The rest go to other private schools, some of them profit-making.

Evidence from the Oxford Social Mobility Study[32] has shown that 67 per cent of the pupils at public schools come from the most affluent 14 per cent of homes; and that nearly nineteen out of twenty come from middle-class or upper-class backgrounds. Only 6 per cent of public school pupils come from the working-class families that make up 55 per cent of the population. The average proportion of working-class children at other private schools is somewhat higher – about 11 per cent – but this is marginal when compared with comprehensives (60 per cent) or even state grammar schools (37 per cent).

Fees make up most of the income at most private schools. Research undertaken for the Public Schools Commission estimated that 92 per cent of the income at the average public school was derived from fees and related charges.[33] This was in 1965, but the proportion is unlikely to have decreased; nor is it likely to be less at other private schools, most of which are not well endowed. Most of the fee income at private schools is paid by pupils' families but central and local government contribute something of the order of 10 per cent. Local authorities spent £32 million in 1980/81 buying places in private schools for non-handicapped pupils. Central government spent over £50 million in the same year for the children of diplomats and military personnel and also began the assisted places scheme at a cost of around £5 million.

Private fee-paying dominates the picture; and charitable endowments are relatively insignificant at most private schools. The Public Schools Commission research – the only reliable evidence in this field – estimated endowments at only 3 per cent of total income at the average public school, although it pointed out that use of capital assets for such purposes as free housing for teachers provided, in effect, a further 2 per cent of notional endowment income.[34] A few schools had sizeable endowments but fewer than one in ten had an endowment greater than 10 per cent of overall income and only at one in thirty was it greater than 25 per cent.

These charitable trusts are put to a variety of quite distinct uses. At one extreme, a limited number of schools preserve the ancient tradition of providing free places for poor children. At Christ's Hospital, Horsham, for example, fees may be paid entirely out of the endowment, subject to a stringent means test, and others, such as Reed's School, Cobham, and Lord Wandsworth College, Basingstoke, take a similar line. At the other extreme some schools use their endowment merely to mitigate fees to all parents, most of whom are not poor by any reckoning. But the most common practice seems to be the provision of scholarships and bursaries which rarely, however, amount to even as much as 50 per cent of the fees charged; and as the Public Schools Commission observed,

> Many of these awards are not related to parental income, but to academic merit. They are seldom large enough to bring in pupils of an income group appreciably lower than would normally be represented in the school. Their purpose is not to meet needs but to attract the best pupils. Although changes have recently been made in the scholarship examinations at certain well-known schools, most awards can only be competed for successfully by pupils who have specialised early in the examination subjects at preparatory schools familiar with the requirements. Thus although the intention of some benefactors may have been to provide opportunities for poor boys, free or assisted places provided through endowment income are seldom open to pupils regardless of means.[35]

The other effect of private schools' charitable status is the exemption from various kinds of taxation and other public levies. This is not huge: it is generally accepted by all concerned that fees would not increase by more than 10 per cent if the concessions were not available; and since the annual rise in fees at many schools has averaged as much or more than this in recent years, loss of tax exemptions is something that nearly all schools and parents could take in their stride. And unlike endowment income, which is sometimes concentrated on helping poor children, the benefit of tax concessions accrues equally to all fee-payers, regardless of their wealth.

The inescapable general conclusion is that the charitable status accorded to all non-profit-making private schools is markedly regressive in its distribution of charitable resources and privileges. With a few important exceptions, it does virtually nothing to benefit the less well-off. The courts seem to accept that middle-class families are 'a sufficiently important section of the public' to meet their criteria for charitable status. But is this historical and accidental legacy sound public policy today? Not, as mentioned earlier, in the view of the Labour Party nor the SDP nor the Liberals. Before considering this issue, however, a brief glance at charity in the field of non-state medicine may be useful.

CHARITY AND HEALTH CARE

Vociferous in its desire to sweep away private education, the Labour party is strangely silent when it comes to charitable status for private health care. Cynics will point to the labour movement's Achilles heel: the Manor House and Inverforth House Hospitals. These are funded by trades union subscriptions and although traditionally they specialised in treating industrial disease, they now offer a general range of hospital services for the labour movement. But this embarrassment is not the only reason for socialist hesitation.

The history of non-statutory medicine in some ways resembles that of the public schools but there are important differences. Medical need is often urgent and British doctors, bound by the Hippocratic oath, had a long tradition of charging what they believed a patient could afford, if anything. So the poor never became excluded from medical care to anything like the same extent as in education and many Victorian charitable hospitals were still dedicated entirely to healing the poor sick. A second major difference is that whereas only a handful of public schools have ever joined the state education system, the great majority of voluntary hospitals were absorbed by the new National Health Service in 1948. A minority remained independent, however, and today the 136 members of the Association of Independent Hospitals and Kindred Organisations run some 200 hospitals, nursing homes and clinics.[36] Most members (70 per cent) are charities and they account for 83 per cent of the 13,000 beds provided by members of the Association.

And among the hospital charities, the tradition of providing access to all, regardless of means, is much stronger than in private education. Well over half those listed in the Association's *Yearbook* either offer their services entirely free; or provide free places for people on low incomes; or require only a nominal annual subscription; or receive much of their income from the NHS on an agency basis. Many are not the up-market establishments one might expect. A number, for instance, are run by the Sisters of Mercy with a tradition of service going back to Florence Nightingale and at the London *Hospital of St John and St Elizabeth* 'the sick poor are nursed free of charge but patients who are able to do so are asked to contribute according to their means'. Then there are the *hospices*, pioneering new approaches to the care of the dying, where no patient is excluded because of lack of financial resources; and a variety of other specialist agencies meeting needs served inadequately, if at all, by the NHS.

That said, there are also more than a few 'charitable' hospitals, nursing homes and clinics which resemble private education much more closely. The most striking example, perhaps, is the Nuffield Nursing Home Trust established in 1957 by BUPA (the British United Provident Association) 'to promote and encourage the provision of modern hospitals for the acute surgical and medical treatment of private patients'. This charitable trust, which now runs thirty-two hospitals funded almost entirely by payments from the BUPA insurance schemes, has as its beneficiaries those prepared to pay BUPA's subscriptions, which, although not huge, must be beyond the means of most people on low incomes: an old-age pensioner couple in London, for example, would have to find nearly £700 a year.

As with public schools, the effect on this type of charitable hospital of losing tax exempt status would be marginal and not likely to deter many BUPA subscribers, most of whom appear to be middle-class people seeking to avoid the long queues and general inconvenience that mars so much of NHS provision.

A SUFFICIENT SECTION OF THE PUBLIC?

To return to 'public benefit'. Is a clientele consisting largely of middle-class pupils or patients with a few token working-class representatives a 'sufficiently important section of the public' to meet the criteria for charitable status? The *Macduff* case quoted at the beginning of this chapter established what might be called the *Macduff Test*: that no trust can be charitable which excludes the poor. It is often suggested, however, that this does not imply that any attempt must be made to provide benefits to the poor but only that every charity must, like the Park Lane Hilton, be open *in principle* to poor applicants even if most or all of them are *in practice* excluded by their inability to pay.

This may well be so; but it does not necessarily follow that charities which in practice exclude the poor are entitled to tax and rating concessions. The *Income and Corporation Taxes Act 1970*, like its predecessors, specifies not only that the *purposes* of a trust must be exclusively charitable but also that the income must be *applied* for charitable purposes only; and other relevant legislation such as the *General Rate Act 1967* contains similar provisions. The Inland Revenue takes this to mean that where a trust is charitable in law, it may not apply its income in non-charitable ways and this view has been upheld by the Court of Appeal. This principle – which might be called the *Metal Box rule* – was established in a case brought by the Revenue against a charity established by the Metal Box Company to provide educational grants and bursaries.[37] The charity's declared purposes made no mention of any special relationship with the Metal Box Company, doubtless because a trust to provide education for the children of company employees cannot be charitable.[38] In practice, however, for several years more than 75 per cent of the charity's income was applied to grants to Metal Box children. There was nothing illegal about this – the grants were *intra vires* the charity's purposes – but the courts accepted that the income had not been *applied* to charitable purposes.

The Metal Box decision demonstrates that trusts with exclusively charitable purposes but which apply a proportion of their income to non-charitable purposes will be allowed to retain their charitable status but will lose the tax relief on the income that is not used charitably. If the *Macduff test* applied to such situations – and it would be a strange logic that did not so apply it – one would expect that charities whose benefits extended to the poor in principle, yet which excluded them in practice, would remain charities but lose tax-exempt status. However, the combined effect of the Macduff test and the Metal Box rule has never been tested in the courts. The Inland Revenue could bring a test case if they chose, but show no signs of wishing to do so. They are not, however, the only party able to take up the issue: a local authority could bring an action to enforce rate payments and the following hypothetical example illustrates the issues involved.

LONDON BOROUGH OF BENNVILLE v. HAYEK FOUNDATION TRUSTEES

The Hayek Foundation, a charity registered in 1975, administers a school and a small hospital in the London Borough of Bennville. The Borough, having unsuccessfully sought payment of rates at 100 per cent, brought an action to enforce such payment. The plaintiffs did not dispute that the Foundation's establishments were open in principle to poor children and poor patients. But they claimed that as the fees at the school were over £2,000 per annum; and as the annual subscription to the provident association linked to the hospital ranged from £200 for a single person under 30 to £750 for a couple over the age of 65; and as there were no concessions or bursaries for low-income applicants; that in practice the facilities were used only by well-to-do people and that taking into account the *Macduff test* (no purpose is charitable which excludes the poor) the use made of the premises was not wholly or mainly charitable and so did not qualify for rate relief under the *General Rate Act 1967*.

The defence entered by the Foundation conceded that the premises were used mainly by well-to-do people but raised eight objections in point of law. Each is summarised with the counter-objections of the plaintiffs' reply printed in italics.

1. The *Pemsel* case[39] established the principle that tax concessions are available to all charities, not just those relieving poverty. *The truth lies somewhere in between. As Lord Macnaghten said, trusts other than those for the relief of poverty 'are not the less charitable in the eye of the law because incidentally they benefit the*

rich as well as the poor'.[40] *Incidentally benefiting the rich as well as the poor is not the same thing as benefiting mainly the well-off.*

2. The *Lonsdale* case (a school for the sons of gentlemen)[41] established that educational trusts can exclude the working class in principle. *The sons of gentlemen may be poor; but by no means every middle-class male is a gentleman nor every working man rough, as the old phrase 'one of nature's gentlemen' reminds us; and the presence of the title over a public amenity excludes no man who can afford the nominal penny.*

3. The *Abbey, Malvern Wells* case[42] established that all schools of learning, whatever the fees they charge, are charities unless they are profit-making.[43] *Not all non-profit-making schools are charitable: a school to teach golf, for instance, could not be a charity, nor could a school for the sons of millionaires. The issue is not whether fees are charged but whether this excludes low-income pupils. And if a trust's purposes do not benefit a sufficiently important section of the public they are in law not charitable purposes even though the benefits conferred are of the very character stated in the 1601 preamble.*[44]

4. In the *Campbell College* case[45] the House of Lords established beyond a doubt that 'education is charitable in its own right' regardless of whether there is any relief of poverty.[46] *With the greatest of respect for Lord Radcliffe, this cannot be deduced from the Pemsel case. In any event, the Campbell College decision was in no way concerned with this question: the issue at stake was the interpretation of the* Valuation (Ireland) Amendment Act 1854.

5. As the law now stands aged, sick and disabled people need not be poor to be entitled to charitable relief: the words in the 1601 preamble 'aged, impotent and poor' are to be read disjunctively.[47] *This is not settled beyond a doubt: the issue has never gone to the House of Lords who could decide the words should be read conjunctively. But in any case, not to confine a hospital's care to the poor is quite different from effectively excluding them.*

6. To extend the Metal Box rule to remove tax exemption from institutions which few low-income people can afford, would overturn long-standing precedents upsetting arrangements on which thousands of people rely. *The available evidence shows that to do this would have only a marginal effect on fees at all but a very few institutions. And longevity of precedents is no sound reason in itself to preserve them. As Lord Wilberforce has said 'I cannot accept the suggestions that because a rule is long established only legislation can change it.'*[48]

7. Both the school and the hospital indirectly confer a benefit on the wider public (a) by making their pupils and patients healthier and wiser, (b) by relieving public expenditure to the extent that would be needed if they relied upon statutory provision and (c) by shortening queues at state hospitals. There is sound authority from the *Re Resch* case[49] that (b) and (c) adequately meet the criterion of sufficient public benefit. *With the greatest of respect for Lord Wilberforce, it is submitted that his reasoning in Re Resch was dubious and the case wrongly decided. Certainly the argument cannot apply to education: a trust to educate dozens of the children of employees at a commercial firm is not charitable[50] and the fact that the general public indirectly benefits has, on great authority, been held not to confer the necessary public element.[51] And that being so it is far from obvious why it should apply to health care.[52]*

8. The hospital's research into back pain and the school's endeavours in the field of curriculum development are widely respected. This provides an additional element of wider public benefit. *Such activites may well be acceptable 'applications of income to charitable purposes'. But they cannot redeem parallel activities: a charity's purposes must be exclusively charitable and for the purpose of rate relief, premises must be used wholly or mainly for charitable purposes.*

So much for the claims, objections and counter-objections. What might be the outcome? A definitive answer could only come from the House of Lords, so let us assume that whichever party lost at first instance appealed. What would be the decision of their lordships? Difficult to predict, but assume for the sake of argument that at least one of them – let us call him Lord Donne – was something of an amateur historian well versed in Tudor and Stuart law.

THE CANON OF MISCHIEF

Lord Donne might begin his speech by recalling the long-established canons of statutory interpretation of which there are three:

1. The literal rule: the words in the statute mean literally what they say and must be followed literally.

2. The golden rule: if a literal interpretation leads to a manifest

absurdity which the courts believe Parliament cannot have intended, an alternative interpretation which avoids the absurdity may be adopted.

3. The mischief rule, or canon of mischief: if neither of the first two rules produces a reasonable result, the courts may determine what to do by identifying the mischief which the statute was enacted to deal with and decide the case in accordance with this purpose.

He would then go on to consider how these applied to the Statute of 1601 as it bore on *London Borough of Bennville v. Hayek Foundation Trustees*. He might conclude that the phrase 'aged, impotent and poor' must be construed conjunctively since otherwise the result would be the absurdity of rate relief for what were, in effect, services almost exclusively for the well-to-do.

More importantly, he would go on to consider what the mischief was that the 1601 Act sought to prevent. He would find clues in the fact that it formed a small part of the wider poor-law legislation and in the preamble to its predecessor of 1597 which states that charitable funds 'have been and are still like to be most unlawfully and uncharitably converted to the lucre and Gayne of somme fewe greedy and covetous persons'. But he would rely also on Francis Moore's *Reading* with its indisputable evidence that a purpose was to be charitable in law only if it either benefited the poor or, if that was unavoidable, the rich as well, but not the well-to-do alone.

Donne, L.J. would doubtless decide that it would upset too much established and often useful case law to contemplate entirely restoring these stringent requirements; but he would find persuasive authority in the Macduff, Pemsel and other decisions that, while any charitable trust may benefit the rich as well as the poor even when to do so is avoidable, a trust which primarily or entirely benefits the well-off can only be charitable in exceptional circumstances, which do not include those of the establishments provided by the Hayek Foundation.

He would go on to hold that the *Metal Box rule* applied to any charity which *intra vires* applied its funds to purposes which failed to benefit a sufficient section of the community and to conclude that the Hayek Foundation should retain its charitable status but pay its rates.

THE WIDER ISSUES

Is it likely that a majority of the Law Lords would hold this view? Possibly not, especially if the case was brought by the London Borough of Bennville which after all would only reduce its rates bill by a fractional amount. But let us imagine Lord Justice Donne concludes his speech with a few general observations on the wider issues.

'It is one thing to hold that schools and hospitals which exist primarily to serve the needs of the well-to-do should pay the same rates and taxes as they would were they not charities. It is quite another to suggest that they should be abolished altogether. Let me concentrate on education.

'First, abolition of private schools would be expensive. It is generally accepted that it would cost not much less than £200 million; it could be considerably more. Now I cannot accept the argument that such a sum is prohibitively expensive but one does have to face the question, "With so many unsatisfied demands for social welfare, might not such a sum be better spent on some other purpose?" The answer given by the abolitionists would, I imagine, be that by cutting the roots of economic and social privilege, the long-term social welfare benefit would greatly outweigh the short-term financial cost.

'But are private schools the roots of economic and social privilege? Do they *create* class divisions or do they merely *reflect* them? I do not doubt that they contribute to some degree to the perpetuation of privilege but one has only to look abroad to realise that they cannot be its chief cause. The élite in France, in the USA – even in Russia – is educated almost entirely at state schools; yet it no more (and no less) recruits from humble homes than does the élite in this country. One cannot ignore how researchers have shown, time and again, that what the school does, while by no means insignificant, has far less impact on academic achievement than the values and habits inculcated in the home. Or as Osbert Sitwell put it: "I was educated in the holidays from Eton".

'Moreover, even if private schools were abolished, well-to-do parents would find ways of ensuring that their children obtained the best education available. Already, since the decline of the grammar school, one has seen a good deal of this: who does not know convinced middle-class socialists who have moved house, at great expense, merely to be in the catchment area of a 'good' comprehensive? And, paradoxically, this exacerbates social divisions by increasing residential segregation. One might I suppose abolish the right to freedom of movement, introducing controls over where people could live. But in reality, the roots of economic and social privilege lie in income differentials and inherited wealth and the abolitionists might do well to consider Nye Bevan's prescient observation: "I do not favour private education, but I would not prohibit it. ... Different levels of income will always find expression in different standards of education".

'To seek to abolish private schools without abolishing differences in income and wealth may well be futile. But to seek reform is another matter: a stick and carrot approach could well help edge a number of schools towards meeting a much wider range of need. I have not favoured the *Metal Box rule* on these grounds – it is not the function of judges to reform society – but because in my view, it is the correct application of the law. Nevertheless, it does create a small stick and a small carrot, as would a selective application of VAT to private school fees. But stick *without* carrot will miss opportunities: there are more than a few in the private sector like the late Sir Robert Birley (a former headmaster of Eton) who favour the closer integration of private schools with the state system. Exemption from rates and taxation for schools which are genuinely striving towards serving the community as a whole, could well strengthen their hand. Some schools might become useful sixth-form colleges, for instance, or even high-class neighbourhood comprehensives.

'Those who believe in the state's responsibility for education will feel that chance should not be lost, arguing that private schools are not the most serious problem in our education system, however objectionable some may find them. They will see the real problem as the inadequacy of substantial parts of what the state provides. Don't misunderstand me, there are many excellent comprehensives as good as anything in the private sector. But there is also a substantial minority of gravely substandard schools, particularly in inner-city areas.

'There is little public support for abolition of private schools: opinion polls consistently find around 90 per cent of voters opposed to it, including a clear majority among Labour voters. That might be put down to what some sociologists would call "false consciousness"; but it may also reflect dissatisfaction with what the state provides both in terms of quality and lack of choice. Surely something has gone awry when two out of three parents in the London Borough of Hackney – one of the most deprived inner-city areas in the country – want alternative schools provided within the comprehensive system?[53]

'You can, of course, assume that the public are naive and misguided and do not have anything useful to say about their children's education. Or you may reject such paternalist assumptions and hold that improving quality and choice within the state system is the real challenge facing British educators and politicians. And if you give that need a high priority, and if £200 million could be put towards meeting it, how could you divert the money to paying for the education of children from well-to-do homes?

'If such decisions had to be faced in real life, I do not doubt that common sense would prevail over ideology. What I find far more worrying, is that when that moment eventually arrived, the decision makers would not have pondered how to use £200 million to do anything constructive about the problems haunting innumerable anxious parents from every kind of background. But then, of course, that moment may not ever arrive. For although it may be possible to flog symbolic stalking horses to a naive minority, *dead* horses cannot substitute for policies – you cannot fool all of the public all of the time.'

6. Building a New Society

The role of the charity is to bind up the wounds of society. This is what they get their fiscal privileges for. To build a new society is for someone else.

(Terence FitzGerald)[1]

Bassiano: *And I beseech you,*
Wrest once the law to your authority;
To do a great right, do a little wrong,
And curb this cruel devil of his will.
Portia: *It must not be. There is no power . . .*
Can alter a decree established:
'Twill be recorded for a precedent
And many an error by the same example
Will rush into the state. It cannot be.

(The Merchant of Venice)[2]

It is hard to believe that Mr Fitzgerald, the recently retired Chief Charity Commissioner, can really have viewed charities' role as confined to covering up society's running sores. The Commissioners have, after all, found no difficulty in registering charities whose purpose is the *prevention* of injury rather than the application of sticking plasters – family planning clinics, for example, or ASH (Action on Smoking and Health). Nor is it easy to see why the whole category of educational purposes should be classified as bandages.

Indeed, it is something of a cliché that charities have always been among the chief pioneers responding to the new attitudes and problems thrown up by economic and social change, often leading the way in meeting new needs and developing new ways of meeting long-established needs. How far contemporary social policy should build on this tradition is a complex question which goes beyond the scope of the present study.[3] But whatever policies are adopted by central or local government, pioneering voluntary organisations will continue to spring up wherever people are unsatisfied with what the state provides. The important question in the present context is how adequately the law is able to develop its concept of charity to allow new forms of voluntary action to qualify for charitable status.

Over the centuries the Court of Chancery granted charitable

status to a host of purposes undreamed of in 1601; and the courts still retain substantial discretion to continue this tradition. As Chief Chancery Master, R. E. Ball, has written.:

> It is my personal belief that the concept of the trust has not yet by any means reached its evolutionary terminus and that it may react with advancing human consciousness to produce increasing realisation of man's place in the scheme of things. Hopeful signs are the growing awareness of responsibility for the environment, the dangers of pollution, the duty of protecting the animal and vegetable kingdoms and the need to investigate the extrasensory. Trusts may be formed to deal with all these things. The more man can be made to feel himself to be a trustee not merely for his family, the locality, the nation or even humanity but for the planet in its totality or eventually even for areas outside the planet (not necessarily in a three-dimensional sense), the more nearly will he approach to the realisation of his destiny. There is no reason to suppose that the law of trusts, including that of charitable trusts, will find any difficulty in consolidating the foundations needed to turn these flights of fancy into actuality.[4]

A remarkable vision. But, without wishing to challenge in any way its admirable depth, it must be said that anyone familiar with the recent history and developing character of the voluntary movement will wonder how far it is able to accommodate the plans and aspirations of many of the groups which have emerged in the last twenty years or so. Does it, for instance, encompass any of what Robert Holman has described as 'the proliferation of community action groups such as tenants' associations, claimants unions, housing action centres, community bodies, residents organising day care, play schemes and so on, whose aggressiveness, determination and class consciousness has added a new dimension to voluntary work'[5]? Or self-organised community nurseries, disabled mutual aid groups, allotment societies, black supplementary schools, women's aid centres, gay counselling services, tenants' co-operatives, community bookshops and cyclists' action groups? For as Ken Worple has said:

> Voluntary activity is less and less about flag days, 'hospital days' and the home visiting of the poor by the leisured religious wealthy. It's more and more about self-organisation and mutual aid, often by particular groups of consumers politically aware of the shortcomings of state

services. Before the war there were only specialist organisations for the deaf and blind. Today there are thousands of single-issue organisations, involving millions of people in fund-raising, pressure group politics, and, perhaps most importantly, active and self-respecting mutual aid.[6]

The present head of the judiciary, Lord Hailsham, recently said that 'the legal conception of charity (is) not static, but moving and changing' and this is undoubtedly correct; but is it 'moving and changing' quickly enough and in the most helpful direction? What follows briefly surveys some of the areas where difficulties seem to occur.

CHILDREN IN CARE

The extent to which the legal conception of charity can move and change depends to a considerable extent on the courts' past decisions. A court can refuse to follow decisions made by inferior courts but the Charity Commissioners, being at the bottom of the hierarchy, have no such freedom.

One much-criticised precedent is the 1958 decision by the Court of Appeal that a trust for the general benefit and welfare of children in care is not charitable. The intended beneficiaries of the bequest in *Re Cole*[7] were the children at a local authority home. The home catered for 'deprived' children: orphans and other children whose parents were held incapable of providing a suitable upbringing; and 'delinquents': juvenile offenders and children held to be out of control or uncontrollable.

The Court of Appeal has since been taken not to have approved the decision at first instance which ruled that such children and such a home were not valid objects of charity.[8] But the Court nevertheless disallowed the bequest on the grounds that the general benefit of such children could be interpreted in such a way as to allow the purchase of amenities not essential for their welfare. Specific examples were given of such 'luxuries': a television set or a gramophone and records.[9]

This somewhat ungenerous decision is often contrasted with the courts' more sympathetic treatment of the needs of public school pupils as, for instance, in decisions holding charitable gifts to build squash courts at Aldenham School[10] and a swimming pool at Marlborough.[11] As Professor Chesterman writes, when such decisions are compared with the *Re Cole* case:

The inequity in charity law's response to the provision of recreation amongst children in different social classes becomes painfully obvious. Trusts to provide recreational and other amenities for orphans and other disadvantaged children at what are likely to be cheerless and under-equipped council homes are held non-charitable because there is no 'charity' in providing actual or potential delinquents with television sets. On the other hand, the only reason why Marlborough College could not have a swimming pool and hot baths built for it in accordance with the terms of a charitable trust was that it already possessed these.[12]

It is generally believed that the House of Lords would overturn this curious ruling but meanwhile the 'dead hand' of precedent has prevented subordinate courts (and presumably the Charity Commissioners) from allowing trusts for the benefit of children in care.[13]

INFORMATION, ADVICE AND COUNSELLING

British citizens are entitled to a wide range of services and benefits and enjoy a variety of legal rights such as protection against unfair dismissal from employment. Few of us completely understand the complexities of all this – what our rights are, what forms to fill in and where to send them, what organisations can provide help etc., etc. – nor is there much point in mastering it all since much of it will never affect us. When a problem does arise, however, some of us may be able to work out for ourselves what to do but many would be lost without a reliable source of information and advice. And many services exist to meet this need.

The public benefit of providing such a service seems fairly obvious yet advice-giving is not in law a charitable purpose. The leading authority for this is a Commonwealth appeal where the Privy Council held that an organisation founded to provide advice on domestic, health etc. matters was not charitable.[14] It must, of course, be admitted that there would be dangers in allowing every kind of advice-giving to be charitable: nobody, one imagines, would want to see non-profit-distributing firms of tax consultants entitled to tax concessions. So some kind of restriction is inevitable. The most common way round the problem used today is to make advice-giving a *means* to some other, charitable *end*. Thus it is quite legitimate to provide advice services to groups which themselves are valid objects of charity – the poor, the sick and so on. But not to provide advice and information as an end in itself. With good legal advice this approach can often provide a solution, although the resulting official 'purposes' are often an extremely artificial way of describing the objectives of the charity. But this does not always work, particularly if a would-be charity imagines it can do without professional legal help. A case study may be helpful to illustrate the point.*

The Highrise Advice Centre, Loamshire, is situated in a neighbourhood consisting almost entirely of council housing and many of the residents have relatively low incomes although not all could be described as poor. About half the centre's work involves problems to do with social security benefit but rent and hire-purchase arrears, matrimonial and housing problems, neighbour complaints, redundancies and cases of unfair dismissal are also common. Clients are also represented at Supplementary Benefit, Industrial and Rent Tribunals. The centre was offered a grant by a charitable foundation but to receive this it needed to become a registered charity. Not anticipating any difficulty the chairman of the management committee did not seek legal advice but applied directly to the Charity Commission. After replying to a request for further information he received the following response:

Dear Sir
HIGHRISE ADVICE CENTRE LOAMSHIRE
Thank you for your letter and enclosures dated 30 July 1981.
I have studied the information you have forwarded pertaining to the activities of the Centre, but I regret to inform you that I could not recommend the registration of the Centre as a charity. Insofar as the Centre assists members of a charitable class, for instance those in need or disabled or sick, by the giving of advice or assistance in legal matters, or educates the public at large, the work of the Centre could be regarded as charitable whereas the giving of advice or legal assistance generally would not be. In view of these doubts and the lack of any evidence that the proposed constitution does not accurately reflect the activities of the Centre, I am not in a position to offer assistance nor do I deem it necessary to go into greater detail at this stage. If you consider that there are other

*This is a real case but at the advice centre's request its name has been fictionalised to preserve anonymity.

factors which have not so far been taken into account or
matters change in the future, it is always open to you to ask
for the question to be reconsidered.

In short, if all the clients had been poor (rather than just most of
them) there would have been no problem in construing the
Centre's purposes as charitable. It seems a little ironic that a
minority of clients who are not poor should rule out charitable
status when hospitals for private patients, from which the poor are
effectively excluded by expensive fees, are not debarred.

There are, in fact, ways round this, as the charitable status of
many Citizen's Advice Bureaux demonstrates. But clearly this
area of the law leaves a great deal to be desired. A related problem
is the difficulty that some organisations have encountered in
relation to providing 'counselling' services but the issues at stake
are more or less the same.

UNEMPLOYMENT

With over three million people out of work it is not surprising that
most people see unemployment as 'the most urgent problem
facing the country at the present time'.[15] The misery of idleness,
the impoverishment of families and the loss of confidence and
self-respect are worrying enough. Still more disturbing is the
growing evidence that problems such as physical and mental
illness, baby battering, suicide, serious crime and even rioting,
increase as unemployment rises.

Nobody will disagree that the fundamental answers to this
worsening problem must be sought primarily in the realm of
economic policy. But a charitable spirit cannot easily stand aside
and ignore the suffering that unemployment brings. So, as one
might expect, a great many voluntary and community organisations are seeking ways of tackling employment problems.
Through community-based projects some are helping to create
new jobs and provide training opportunities and work experience
for unemployed people. Others have taken up an educational role,
developing adult education, skills training and retraining, and
pre-employment work with young people.

The public benefit of much of this might seem too obvious to
need much justification. Yet the relief of unemployment is said
not to be, in law, a charitable purpose. The courts have yet to

consider the point but the Charity Commission takes the view that

> The unemployed become an object of charity only when they are also poor or otherwise in need. It follows that it is not open to a charity to appeal for funds, or to apply funds, for the benefit of those whose only common feature is that they are without work.[16]

The underlying logic is not unreasonable: why should a trust for the benefit of, say, lazy film stars enjoy the privileges of charitable status? Yet the fact that a hospital for sick actors could benefit wealthy screen idols is no impediment to its gaining charitable status. And there is ample evidence that the great majority of unemployed people are anything but affluent.

As with advice-giving the issue is partly no more than a matter of semantics and the logic of means and ends. You may feel it makes your trust deeds a rather artificial description of what you are trying to do; but however antiquated the terminology, provided you are able to present your proposed relief of unemployment as a *means* of achieving some other, accepted charitable purpose rather than as an *end* in itself, the obstacles will melt away.

> The relief of poverty among unemployed persons is clearly a charitable purpose and, insofar as an institution is assisting people to find employment as a means of relieving their poverty, there would be no difficulty in the institution obtaining registration.[17]

There is clear authority in the 1601 preamble for such thinking; in particular there are the words 'The supportation, aid and help of young tradesmen, handicraftsmen and persons decayed.' This has always been held to subsume apprenticeships and the provision of tools, stock and loans for young people setting up in business. The Elizabethan notion was quite wide: 'persons decayed' were not merely sick people: Sir Francis Moore's *Reading* shows that 'decay' had a much wider reference. For example,

> To pay the fees for bankrupts to go out of prison to meet with their creditors, is a charitable use within the statute, for it is the relief of persons decayed.[18]

And if the relief of bankruptcy is a charitable purpose it seems fairly clear that 'the supportation, aid and help' of those who cannot support themselves was intended to cover a fairly wide range of assistance. So, for example, 'to buy stock to assist tradesmen' was charitable and although Moore is careful to point out that the main purpose of such a gift must be to aid 'young tradesmen and persons decayed', he also repeatedly makes the point that 'if the poor cannot be relieved without benefiting the rich, the rich also in this unseverable case will benefit by being counted with the poor'.[19] Where this was avoidable, the seventeenth-century commissioners could insist that a trust should support only the young and 'person decayed' but they were not bound to do so.

Our latter-day Charity Commissioners, however, seem to take a more restrictive view, insisting that *only* the poor may benefit:

> Much as we deprecate the extent and effects of unemployment, the fact remains that helping to finance the establishment of a commercial organisation to provide employment is not in itself a charitable application of funds. The unemployed people who might be taken on would not necessarily be poor and, even if they were, the benefit accruing to them would be secondary and indirect compared with the financial benefit accruing to the organisation, whose profits would presumably be shared by all the legal owners who, even in a workers co-operative, are unlikely all to be poor.[20]

In line with this they currently refuse to allow most trusts for job-creation as opposed to vocational training. The Northamptonshire Rural Community Council, for example, recently applied to register a trust to establish four small factory units to be let for a maximum of eighteen months, at low cost, to new enterprises. The Charity Commission replied that

> It appears that the purpose of the workshops is to enable 'aspiring small businessmen' to start a business of their own. Whilst in the workshops or 'nursery factories' they would be given training and given expert guidance and assistance over the initial setting up period. The purpose appears to be to help individuals to develop businesses so that they may revitalise the economy of the rural community in Northamptonshire. This is not thought to fall within the legal definition of charity. The fact that

educational means are used in part as a method of achieving the purpose is not sufficient to bring it within the educational head of charity. It must I think be considered under the fourth head of charity which are those beneficial to the community in a way that the law considers charitable and it fails here because the benefit to the community is too remote and intangible and is far out-weighed by the benefit to the individuals.[21]

Similar difficulties have been encountered by bodies with more generalised aims. So, as the Charity Commissioners' Report for 1969 records:

A number of industrial development associations have, with government and local authority assistance, been set up throughout the country in areas of high unemployment. There can be no doubt that such organisations are for the general benefit of the community: but the question remains whether this benefit is conferred on the public in a way that is charitable. We received an application for registration as a charity of the Lancashire and Merseyside Industrial Development Association and our first difficulty arose from uncertainty in deciding what were the objects or purposes of the association for, although the association had a number of declared functions, these functions did not seem to us to be purposes in any real sense of that word, nor were they expressed so as to be charitable. Thus the application for the registration of the association has to be rejected. We also considered, however, whether the association might be advised to contemplate adding a statement of objects to its constitution; it would not, of course, have been for us to propound new objects for the association. In discussion we reached the conclusion that there was no clear evidence that its activities and functions could in fact be brought within a series of purposes that were charitable. It would doubtless be possible to arrive at a statement of charitable purposes which would cover part of the work of the association but not the whole of it.[22]

The nature of unemployment problems has, of course, changed dramatically since 1969 and in their annual report for 1980, the Commissioners argued for a flexible approach:

The concept and scope of charities to help the unemployed is still an evolving one and it would be counter-productive for us to attempt to crystallize it prematurely by enunciating fixed principles at this stage. It is preferable to preserve flexibility so that we can, consistently with the law, do as much as possible to help those concerned in their efforts to meet the pressing social need.[23]

And, in some instances, they have fostered a fairly liberal interpretation of existing case law. So, for example, in 1973 they registered as charitable the Clerkenwell Green Association for Craftsmen which, although primarily established to 'encourage the exercise and maintain the standards of crafts both ancient and modern, preserve and improve craftsmanship and foster, promote and increase the interest of the public therein', has seen fit to pursue this goal by, among other things, securing the conversion and acting as manager of a large number of low-rent workshops. To the Inland Revenue this must have seemed the thin edge of a dangerously large wedge, for they appealed to the High Court against the Commissioners' decision. But Mr Justice Fox, in 1980, refused to overturn it. He favoured a distinctly liberal construction of the term 'craftsman':

> In the Oxford Dictionary 'craftsmanship' was defined as 'the performance or occupation of a craftsman; skill in clever or artistic work; skilled workmanship'; and 'craft' was defined as, 'an art, trade or profession requiring special skill or knowledge'. 'Craftsmanship' included the activities of a wide range of persons, for example, ordinary glaziers, cabinet makers, bookbinders, jewellers, etc. As a practical matter, it seemed to him that difficulties in determining the ambit of crafts or craftsmanship were likely to be small.[24]

And went on to say that in his view

> The provision of workshop accommodation for craftsmen in London, bearing in mind the evidence as to the difficulty of obtaining such accommodation, must encourage the exercise of craftsmanship; and, since without suitable accommodation the activity itself might wither, it would help to maintain standards, more particularly, perhaps, in enterprises like Cornwall House and Pennybank Chambers which produced a concentration of craftsmen. But was this charitable? He considered *Inland Revenue Commissioners v. Yorkshire Agricultural Society* [1928] I.K.B. 611, *In re. Town and Country Planning Act, 1947; Crystal Palace Trustees v. Minister of Town and Country Planning* [1951] Ch. 132 and *Construction Industry Training Board v. Attorney-General* [1971] 1 W.L.R. 1303 and said that these

cases seemed to him to establish that the promotion or advancement of industry (including a particular industry such as agriculture) or of commerce is a charitable object provided that the purpose is the advancement of the benefit of the public at large and not merely the promotion of the interests of those engaged in the manufacture and sale of their products. In his opinion, the fact that individual craftsmen might obtain benefits from the Association's activities was not conclusive on the question of charitable status.[25]

This valuable test case was made possible by the Inland Revenue's admirable willingness to pay all the Association's legal costs as well as their own and is an excellent model for the development of charity law: the Commissioners taking a liberal view, chivalrously opposed by the Inland Revenue with its responsibility to the taxpayer. It seems a pity that the Commissioners do not feel able to extend this approach to other areas where the boundaries of what is charitable are unclear. Even a negative court decision could be helpful inasmuch as it would clearly indicate where legislative amendment might be thought useful. Some lawyers hold the *Crystal Palace* and other decisions just mentioned to allow a wider range of action to tackle unemployment than is currently encouraged; and certainly many will share the view that creating jobs is always preferable to 'charitable' hand-outs, for as the seventeenth-century Quaker reformer, John Bellers, put it:

> It is much more charity to put the poor in a way to live by their own work, than to maintain them idle, as it would be to set a man's broken leg, so he might walk himself, rather than always to carry him.

TRADING BY CHARITIES

At the bottom of many of the problems just discussed is the basic legal premiss that 'trading' is not, as such, a charitable purpose. It is well established that a charity may freely trade if there is some intrinsic connection with its primary purposes: a disabled people's workshop may establish a shop to sell their products; a church may market Bibles and other religious literature; a public school may sell education. But trading which does not in itself advance the charity's primary purposes, is subject to the restriction that it must not dominate the charity's activities. In their annual report of 1980, the Charity Commissioners provided some general guidance on the issue.

> In some cases the trading or other commercial activities may form so small a part of the institution's activities as to be insignificant. In our view trading of this nature would be permissible, but the profits would not enjoy exemption from income tax unless the trading was in the course of carrying out '(i) . . . a primary purpose of the charity, or (ii) the work in connection with the trade is mainly carried out by beneficiaries of the charity' (section 360(1) (e) of the Income and Corporation Taxes Act 1970). At the other end of the scale, trading might dominate the institution's activities to the extent that the trading must necessarily be regarded as a means of providing a livelihood for those carrying it on . . . Between these extremes lies a whole spectrum of cases in which trading plays a smaller or larger part. Drawing the line between the charity which is merely raising funds and furthering its activities by trading and what is in substance a trading institution wearing a charitable mantle is not easy: each case must be considered on its own facts.[26]

Charities often become extremely worried about where exactly the boundary lies between fund-raising and commerce and about whether they should set up non-charitable trading subsidiaries. But the general principle – that charities should not be allowed to trade without paying tax because this would be unfair competition for the ordinary trader – is fairly generally accepted. In the main, the problem is one of adequate advice and information and more might be done to provide this.

Most of the issues of principle arise in connection with unemployment and job-creation. But one other area of contention is the need in some places – mostly remote rural areas but also some inner-city districts – for shops and other services which are not being provided because they would not be commercially viable. The Charity Commissioners seem unwilling, however, to let charities such as Village Halls tackle such problems:

> With the loss in many rural areas of the village shop, the question has arisen whether the provision by voluntary organisations of community shops on a non-profit making basis, possibly staffed by volunteers, would be charitable. Such shops would be of considerable benefit to the elderly, to mothers of young children, to the disabled, and to

families without a car, particularly in those areas where public transport is poor. The establishment of such shops would provide a definite element of benefit to the community, but in our view the benefit is not within a category recognised by law as charitable. The predominant activity of a community shop would be trading, which is essentially a commercial and non-charitable activity; the fact that the institution would be non-profit making, except in the sense that it would have to pay its way, is immaterial.[27]

This rather restrictive interpretation of the law could, of course, be challenged in the courts; but who would pay the considerable costs of such an action?

SELF-HELP AND MUTUAL AID

'Participation' is another area where the risk of private benefit seems to inhibit charity law's capacity to accommodate changing attitudes and problems. Recent years have seen growing support for the idea that ordinary people should have a greater say in the decisions which affect their daily lives and this outlook is increasingly widespread in the voluntary sector. The old idea that people in need should be grateful consumers of services provided by others is gradually giving way to the belief that to reduce people to passive 'clients' risks making them more dependent and incapable of helping themselves and neglects the help they, in turn, may be able to give others. Hence the mushrooming of hundreds of self-help groups and mutual aid schemes.

The legal conception of charity, however, retains a strong emphasis on a distinction between those who provide and those who receive. As Professor Chesterman has written:

> The prohibitions against both profit distribution and 'self-help' clearly originate from a concern to exclude from the privileges attached to charitable status any organisation which confers benefit solely or substantially on those who initiate, subscribe to and control it. In particular, the cases dealing with friendly societies, mutual funds and other similar organisations stress that charity and 'self-help' are opposed concepts.[28]

Perhaps the most common type of self-help groups are those established by and for the sufferers from a variety of disabilities and health problems – Alcoholics Anonymous is one well-known example – and these can qualify as charities provided their benefits are available to anyone in need and not just members of the group. Certain other voluntary groups including neighbourhood and community associations can also gain charitable status. But many are excluded. Professor Chesterman finds this anomalous:

> The outcome, stated bluntly, is that there is one law for the fee-paying school and another for the friendly society . . . Fee-paying schools lack altruism (and also any element of the relief of poverty) in the sense not only that they operate substantially as business concerns providing services in return for fees, but also that they assist in perpetuating the elite position of the social groupings – i.e. the upper and upper middle classes – by which they are funded and maintained . . . By contrast, friendly societies, mutual funds and the like, which operate as defensive mechanisms established traditionally within the working class and lower middle classes to protect against various common misfortunes, are shut out from charitable status because they do not disguise the element of self-help by adopting some more sophisticated form. Such inegalitarian contrasts appear elsewhere in charity law's attitude to altruism . . . Professional associations and even students' unions can sometimes attain charitable status by submerging furtherance of their members' interests into such phrases as 'advancement of education' or 'advancement of surgery', yet a modern style tenants' association formed in a slum area to improve the standards of its members' houses would be shut out by the 'self-help' rule . . . Fee-paying medical clinics without any endowment or other elements of 'giving' may be charitable if they do not distribute profits whereas cooperative health insurance will not be.[29]

The view that this might be something less than equitable cuts across conventional political boundaries. The Conservative MP, Anthony Steen, for example, has said:

> The great danger we face today is that of an apathetic society – witness the soullessness of so many council estates. If we wish to see greater involvement – and our whole ethos since the war has been just that . . . we have got to talk about encouraging community initiatives . . . There is not a very great distinction if you look at the lists of organisations that are so-called charities from those that are not. The distinction is very artificial . . . I know, going up and down

the country, the number of community groups – and I use that to cover a wide spectrum of people involved in bettering their neighbourhood – is very much greater than those who are registered charities. Those who are registered charities get the perks; those that are not, do not. That is the injustice I am trying to rectify ... New thoughts – particularly of this kind – are always threatening, and I do not think we should be too threatened. The Establishment would be very threatened by an idea that would open the floodgates of organisations that could become acceptable. That is what I am trying to get ... groups of people who are 'unacceptable' accepted by the Establishment.[30]

The exclusion of many community groups from tax concessions and rate relief may be unjust but on the whole they survive this handicap. Much sadder is the frequent experience that while applications to charitable trusts and foundations for grants to develop community projects often meet with considerable enthusiasm, funds are nearly always offered on condition that the group becomes a registered charity; and when this proves impossible the project has to be abandoned. In recent years the Charity Commission has moved towards a relatively more liberal construction of existing precedents, as, for example, in the Windmill Hill City Farm case.[31] It could go somewhat further in this direction although even the most liberal construction would not meet the strictures of critics like Chesterman or Steen. That would require legislation.

SELF-MANAGEMENT

If charity begins at home, 'participation' begins at work. A move away from old-fashioned, authoritarian styles of management can be detected in many voluntary organisations. Increasingly employees look to have some say in decisions which can vitally affect their working lives and jobs and at very least they expect a modicum of consultation. But it is only when this trend is carried to its logical conclusion – full 'industrial democracy' – that problems with charity law occur. A growing minority of voluntary organisations are 'self-managing', taking the form of co-operatives or other participative formats.

Those which are charities generally adopt the form of companies limited by guarantee but if they aspire to full 'worker control' they hit a major obstacle. The directors of such a company are its trustees and as a general rule trustees are not allowed to derive any profit from their office. The Charity Commissioners set out their policy on the remuneration of trustees in their 1978 annual report, concluding:

> Shortly, our views are that a power to remunerate trustees is not acceptable, although where there are special reasons remuneration on a reasonable scale within limits set by the governing instrument may be permissible if the trustee or trustees have special qualifications which are not otherwise available to the charity and which would make for its more effective administration. This, however, must always in our opinion be subject to the overriding provision that the number of remunerated trustees must be less than a majority of the quorum and that any such trustees must be absent from meetings and discussions concerning their own appointment, conditions of service and remuneration and must not vote thereon.

The thinking behind this is that if trustees derive a profit from the charity there is an inherent conflict between their own interests and those of the trust's beneficiaries. The theory is that a majority of unpaid, non-worker trustees is necessary to avoid potential abuses.

The notion that forbidding remuneration is likely to deter dishonest trustees from finding ways of lining their own pockets might seem a trifle naive; equally, the idea that those who work for charities can never be trusted to ensure that their own interests do not override those of the beneficiaries is, perhaps, unduly cynical. Nevertheless, unless they change their policy the Charity Commissioners will not allow any out-and-out co-operative to register as a charity. In practice, many co-operatives accept the requirement of what amounts to a non-worker governing board; and, with substantial delegated powers, this can often be a fairly satisfactory solution. Problems can and do occur, however, where board and workers hit some fundamental disagreement over policy which need not have anything to do with the workers' pay.

Other solutions do exist. The Oxford and Cambridge colleges, for example, are self-governing charities with no board of governors. There, the independent assessment of whether the charity is being appropriately managed is provided by the office of 'visitor' who has a fairly wide jurisdiction. And no doubt various other forms of accountability could be devised; for the real issue is not essentially whether or not trustees are paid but whether the charity is properly administered for the public benefit. Case-law precedents do not forbid the exploration of new ways of ensuring public accountability and those who favour the growth of self-management will hope that the Charity Commissioners will be willing to co-operate in carefully monitored experiments. Research into existing innovations in the accountability of social welfare co-operatives could also be useful.

INTERMEDIARY BODIES

It is not only 'self-help' that is frowned on by the law. An attempt by Lord Nuffield to set up a trust to promote the establishment of self-help organisations was held non-charitable[32] notwithstanding the argument that to encourage people to be thrifty and to provide against their own future misfortunes benefited not only them but the public at large.

More generally, organisations which exist to help charities achieve their purposes have often encountered difficulties in obtaining charitable status. So, for example, a county-wide Council for Voluntary Youth Services, which was set up to co-ordinate the activities of local youth clubs etc. in order to achieve a better standard of assistance to young persons in the area, was refused registration on the following grounds:

> I know of no legal authority to support the contention that the mere encouragement of co-operation or co-ordination of activities are within the scope of charitable purposes as recognised by the law. An organisation does not become a charity merely because it sets out to render a service or services to various institutions (albeit charitable institutions) by co-ordinating their activities ... Such an object will not be engaged *directly* in promoting charitable work. It may be that by co-ordinating the activities of charities the better administration and effectiveness thereof is achieved and such activity may be perfectly proper as ancillary to a good charitable object but there exists no legal authority which contends that the co-ordination of activities can stand as a charitable object or purpose in its own right. The results thereof are far too indirect, vague and uncertain.[33]

Or take the case of a county-wide 'Charity Information Service', set up to undertake a review of the need for modernisation among small parochial charities, to set up an information exchange for the local voluntary sector – to bridge the gap between grant-seekers and grant-givers – and to explore the whole field of voluntary giving. This too was told that it could not be registered because it was not itself *directly* involved in the achievement of a charitable purpose:

> Whilst we would not wish to cast any doubt on the value of these services, their provision is not, we think, of itself a charitable purpose. The Commissioners have considered cases of institutions providing services which, though not themselves charitable, are provided exclusively for charities and have considered that such provision is not charitable in the legal sense. So, for example, the provision of a catering service for charities would not itself be charitable (see the Commissioners' Annual Report for 1969 paragraph 20) and we have consistently taken the view that companies established for the sole purpose of acting as trustees or providing other administrative services to charities are not themselves charitable.
>
> It seems to us that this case is very similar; on the basis of the information at present available the proposed institution will not itself advance education, protect health or relieve poverty and sickness (or will not do so as part of its dominant aim) but will be principally concerned with the provision of services enabling other institutions being charities to do so, perhaps more effectively.[34]

One might have thought that the fact that no legal authority existed one way or the other for voluntary bodies which aim to back up the efforts of front-line charities but do not *directly* achieve charitable purposes, would have left the Commission free to register them. Such decisions become still more puzzling when one reflects that many, perhaps even most, national charities provide no direct benefit but exist to promote action by others. The objects of the National Association of Boys' Clubs, for example, are, 'The development of Boys' Clubs throughout the United Kingdom and the provision of specialist help and advice to existing Boys' Clubs.'[35] Or the Housing Associations Charitable Trust: 'To give aid and advice to housing associations affiliated to the National Federation of Housing Associations'.[36] And dozens more examples could be cited.

The report of the Wolfenden Committee, *The Future of Voluntary Organisations*, placed special emphasis on the importance of such development agencies (or intermediary bodies, as they chose to call them) both nationally *and* locally.[37] The Charity Commissioners are currently revising their policy in this area[38] but it remains to be seen how far they will feel able to go.

OTHER AREAS OF CONCERN

Problems seem to occur in a number of other areas. So, for instance, most voluntary bodies concerned with *environmental issues* can be registered as charities, given good legal advice. But the description of their activities in trust deeds often has to be juggled to find an analogy with some decided case. This does, of course, provide a living for lawyers but some people feel that it should be possible to register them more directly. More generally, the need for such juggling acts crops up more often than one might expect and would-be charities are constantly amazed that their eminently charitable intentions have to be dressed up in highly artificial and sometimes archaic terminology to meet the requirements of charity law. This need not be a major problem if expert legal advice is available but many people feel that charitable registration should less often require a battle of wits between solicitors and the Charity Commissioners' legal staff. Moreover, many aspirants to charitable status do not realise that few solicitors possess this particular expertise; and are surprised and dismayed when costly legal help from non-specialists in the field fails to deliver the goods.

'Recreation' is another area where difficulties occur. As Lord Allen said, in a recent House of Lords debate:

> The noble Lord, Lord Goodman, who unfortunately cannot be with us this evening, tells me that in his view the position of sport in relation to charity law is chaotic and that the Sports Council would greatly welcome clarification. He also tells me that the somewhat anaemic Act which was passed in 1958 to deal with recreation is not working well. The Charity Commission, for example, seem to have the idea that the provision of facilities for a single sport does not come within the Act, even if the facilities are open to everybody, because a lot of people may not be interested in that particular sport; and the suggestion is that if this is a correct interpretation of the law as it is then the law needs changing.[39]

The law in this area is not static, however. In 1980 the Lord

Chancellor took the lead in a House of Lords decision overruling the Court of Appeal's refusal to allow a trust to promote soccer at schools and universities. Lord Hailsham rejected the 'dead hand' of precedent, pointing out that

> Both the legal conception of charity, and within it the educated man's ideas about education, are not static, but moving and changing. Both change with changes in ideas about social values. Both have evolved over the years. In particular in applying the law to contemporary circumstances it is extremely dangerous to forget that thoughts concerning the scope and width of education differed in the past greatly from those which are now generally accepted.[40]

The decision left open a number of questions such as whether a trust to promote soccer among adults could qualify as an educational charity. But this generous interpretation of the law should enable the Charity Commissioners to continue to develop a liberal approach. And the decision is a splendid illustration of how a test case pursued to the highest court in the land can help to develop the law of charity to meet changing attitudes and needs.

A rather different aspect of the recreational issue is the question of amateur art. It is clear that 'entertainment' – bingo halls, for example – does not qualify for charitable status which seems reasonable, in principle. But trusts to encourage people to engage in artistic activity rather than remain passive consumers of 'art' sometimes encounter difficulties. So, for instance:

> We are not convinced that the activities of the proposed Trust are concerned with educating the public in the arts, as charity law understands it, and it is not at all obvious that amateur crafts such as silk-screen printing, the technical aspects of photography, murals etc. are 'arts and crafts, both ancient and modern' as we have accepted them. How will the promoters 'preserve and improve craftsmanship'?[41]

In the event, with expert legal advocacy, the Commission was persuaded that the trust was in part educational and in part recreational and could be accepted as long as it did not give help to non-charitable groups such as tenants' associations. The trust has been registered and no doubt, encouraged by Lord Hailsham, the Commission will evolve a less restrictive line.

Problems also occur in relation to fringe medicine. In 1975 the

Charity Commission decided that institutions promoting unorthodox therapies would have to demonstrate that the treatment
had some merit. Established activities such as acupuncture,
osteopathy or faith-healing are unlikely to face many problems,
but less well-known therapies may have to get some backing from
the 'medical profession'. Some will find it a little paradoxical that
the support of the guardians of orthodoxy should be the passport
for the unorthodox.

In contrast, many find it somewhat unjust that while some
fairly bizarre varieties of fringe religion have obtained charitable
status, it is denied to relatively sober humanist trusts. As the
Goodman Committee report put it:

> For many years also there has been concern which has
> recently increased that ethical and moral movements which
> are not founded upon a belief in a deity have not been
> accepted as charitable. An ethical or moral system based on
> agnosticism or atheism clearly cannot fall within any
> definition of religion; yet it may set out to promote the
> moral improvement of mankind which is for the benefit of
> the community. We consider that, in principle, the
> advancement of such movements should be brought within
> the ambit of charity.[42]

And, in this context, it may be worth pointing out that most forms
of Buddhism categorically reject any belief in a deity; yet
Buddhist charities are readily registered.

Finally there is the tangled problem of charitable work
overseas. The major controversy here, which concerns political
activity, is discussed in the next chapter. Less well publicised, but
a problem at times, is that while it is well established that a charity
may apply funds abroad for any purpose falling under the first
three of Lord Macnaghten's heads of charity (i.e. poverty,
education and religion), 'other purposes beneficial to the
community will be charitable only if of benefit to the community
of the United Kingdom'. That, at least, is the Charity
Commissioners' view, as expressed in their annual report for
1963.

Certainly the courts have indicated some restrictions in this
respect. In 1954 Lord Evershed, Master of the Rolls, observed
that:

It may be that on very broad and general grounds, relief of poverty and distress in any part of the world, or the advancement of the Christian religion in any part of the world, would be regarded as being for the benefit of the community in the United Kingdom. I see, however, formidable difficulties, where the objects of the trust were, say, the setting out of soldiers or the repair of bridges or causeways in a foreign country. To such cases the argument of public policy (meaning United Kingdom public policy) might be the answer.[43]

But that is considerably less sweeping than the Commissioners' view in 1963; and it is difficult to see on what legal authority that narrow construction rested. There are signs that the Commission's position is shifting somewhat but difficulties still occur.[44] Many will agree with the Goodman Committee's view that 'no distinction should be drawn between charitable activity by English charities at home and abroad',[45] subject to Lord Evershed's fairly minor restrictions.

And, more generally, their hope 'that it will be possible . . . to bring a more imaginative and positive attitude to bear on the subject of charities'[46] is widely shared. Recently there have been a number of encouraging signs that the Charity Commissioners and the courts are moving towards a more imaginative approach and further progress in that direction could eliminate many of the problems discussed in this chapter. But not all, unless the House of Lords were prepared to exercise their capacity to overrule any precedent rather more freely than seems likely. Some changes would almost certainly require legislation.

7. Charity and Politics

Whoever would overthrow the liberty of a nation must begin by subduing the freeness of speech.

(Benjamin Franklin, 1758)[1]

Charities, whether they operate in this country or overseas, must avoid:
(a) Seeking to influence or remedy those causes of poverty which lie in the social, economic and political structures of countries and communities.
(b) Bringing pressure to bear on a government to procure a change in policies or administrative practices . . .
(c) Seeking to eliminate social, economic, political or other injustice.

(The Charity Commissioners, 1982)[1]

The myth that charities must stay out of politics altogether is surprisingly widespread, even among charities themselves. Yet the courts have made it plain beyond a doubt that by no means all political activity is forbidden to charities. They have also, it is true, clearly defined a limited number of 'no-go' areas. But whether there are any boundaries short of that forbidden territory, and exactly where the frontiers lie, is far from certain.

How far charities may engage in political activity is, in fact, among the most difficult and contentious issues in charity law. There is, in some quarters, the strongly held conviction that charities should be seen and not heard – that the law should, if it does not already, confine charities to providing direct services and financial hand-outs. Others, however, contend that at times *advocacy* may be as important as *service* and that it is not realistic to expect that charities will remain silent when they cannot, for one reason or another, solve a problem simply through their own efforts.

That political activity is in any way incompatible with charity is a fairly recent notion. No clear statement to that effect is known to have been made by the courts before 1917 when Lord Parker ruled that

> The disestablishment of the Church, the secularization of education, the alteration of the law touching religion or

marriage or the observation of the Sabbath, are purely political objects. Equity has always refused to recognize such objects as charitable ... a trust for the attainment of political objects has always been held invalid.[3]

It is possible that had the courts considered the question before 1917 they would have shared Lord Parker's view but the law books show no trace of any such decision; so when he said that the judiciary had 'always refused to recognize such objects as charitable', he considerably overstated how things stood at the beginning of the twentieth century.

For although later judges have followed Lord Parker's dicta, and gradually narrowed charities' scope for political activity, historically charity had not been innocent of political connections. As described in chapter 1, the concept of charity first emerged in the context of a fierce political campaign against social, economic and religious conditions in Ancient Israel. 'Justice' was the principal slogan of that campaign; but when it became clear that even extensive legislative reforms had failed to deliver justice, the campaigners came to insist on a change of heart as well. Charity was not intended, however, to supplant the continuing demands for social justice; it was not to be a substitute for justice but its foundation. Early Christianity made charity the central pivot of its ethical teaching (see chapter 2) and although ecclesiastical institutionalisation has often tended to mute concern for social justice, charity has never entirely lost its radical implications. Perhaps the most striking example of this is the history of slavery.

CHARITY AND THE ABOLITION OF SLAVERY

That any human being could be treated as the property of another, was recognised as an evil by the early Christians; to free a slave was regarded as a 'good work'; slaves could be ordained as priests and several rose to be bishops. Master and slave shared equally in the life of the church. But as Henry Chadwick points out, it was several hundred years before the *abolition* of slavery was seriously contemplated:

> Protests against the institution of slavery as such came in the fourth century when the Christians were beginning to be in a position to affect social policy. But bequests had by this time made the fourth-century Church a considerable landowner, already dependent on endowments for clergy

stipends and therefore in a weak position for initiating economic changes. These protest were too little and too late to revolutionise the economy of the ancient world and only have the historical significance of outlining a programme for the future.[4]

In modern times it was the Quakers who, from 1671, were the first significant opponents of slavery, but by the end of the eighteenth century they were joined by many other religious groupings. The Somersett case in 1772 established that slavery was illegal in Britain, but attempts to abolish the slave trade to the colonies and the USA met with powerful opposition from vested interests. The trade itself was finally made illegal in 1807 but it was not until 1833 that legislation to abolish slavery in the colonies was finally enacted. The campaign had been led by the (largely Quaker) Abolition Society, by the churches and by charities such as the Church Missionary Society. Outside the British Empire, however, slavery continued unabated. In 1839 a new charity was formed – the British and Foreign Anti-Slavery Society – which by keeping up a constant public agitation persuaded successive British governments to take the lead in breaking up the remaining slave trade.

Not many people realise that slavery still exists in some countries even in 1982. And practices similar to slavery remain widespread: debt-bondage, serfdom, forced labour and the sale and exploitation of children. The Anti-Slavery Society is still in existence, still struggling to combat such evils. Today its purposes, as registered with the Charity Commissioners, read:

> The objects of the society are the suppression of slave-owning and slave trading, the abolition of all forms of forced labour approximating to slavery, the protection and advancement of peoples and groups who are not strong enough to protect themselves and the defence of human rights in accordance with the principles of the United Nations Universal Declaration of Human Rights of 1948.

There is little doubt, however, that as the law stands today no new organisation devoted to such ends could be registered as a charity – and strictly speaking the Anti-Slavery Society should be stripped of charitable status. Opposing even the gravest of social injustices – slavery, even genocide – is no longer charitable in the eyes of the law.

The Anti-Slavery Society is not the only registered charity whose status is anomalous. The Howard League for Penal Reform, founded in 1866, has a long history of working for changes in the law and in the administration of prisons; and again, it must be doubtful whether such a body could be registered today. Then there is the Lord's Day Observance Society, long dedicated to opposing any changes in the traditional British Sunday.

POLITICAL ACTIVITY AND THE COURTS

How then has it come about that charities may not have political objects? As already mentioned, the first judge to state that principle was Lord Parker in 1917.

> A trust for the attainment of a political object is not charitable since the Court has no way of judging whether a proposed change in the law will or will not be for the public benefit.[5]

He based this ruling on an obscure case of 1828 where the judge had held that a trust to distribute literature advocating the supremacy of the Pope over secular authority was superstitious, contrary to public policy and not charitable.[6] This was a limited decision – activity contrary to public policy could not be charitable; but influenced by *Tyssen on Charitable Bequests*, an 1888 textbook, Lord Parker transformed it into the much broader principle that no endeavour to change the law in any respect could be a charitable purpose.

The House of Lords did not return to the issue until 1947, when the charitable status of the National Anti-Vivisection Society was challenged by the Inland Revenue.[7] The Law Lords upheld Lord Parker's reasoning – the law cannot judge whether legislation will benefit the public – but promptly contradicted themselves by stating that one reason why anti-vivisectionism could not be charitable was that to ban vivisection would deprive the public of the benefits of an important section of medical research. Clearly the courts can, at times, assess the likely benefit of legislation. The inadequacy of Lord Parker's rule is still more obvious when one looks at examples of its application by the Charity Commission. Take, for example, a letter to a Community Association in which the Commission wrote that,

> The Association has been concerned to act as a pressure group to secure, *inter alia*, a crossing on – Road . . . Seeking to bring pressure to bear to achieve an objective is not a charitable purpose.

One cannot help wondering how many old-age pensioners would need to be knocked down before a court could judge that a pedestrian crossing would be for the public benefit. The Law Lords seem to have been aware, in the 1947 anti-vivisection case, of the difficulties caused by Lord Parker's reasoning, for they added a second argument: that the courts cannot usurp the functions of the legislature and hence cannot hold a political purpose charitable. This argument will be examined later but it is worth noting that their Lordships did emphasise that although an association for promoting legislation cannot be a charity, charitable status is not ruled out if trustees employ political *means* in furthering the *non-political purposes* of a trust.

Lord Porter, in his dissenting judgement, sought to preserve rather more freedom than that. In his view a purpose was only political if it necessitated a change in the law: if it could be achieved by persuasion, at least in principle, then it was not political. Unlike Lord Parker, he had not forgotten the nineteenth-century campaigning charities:

> I cannot accept the view that the anti-slavery campaign or the enactment of the Factory Acts, or the abolition of the use of boy labour to sweep chimneys would be charitable so long as the supporters of these objects had not in mind or, at any rate, did not advocate a change in the laws but became political and therefore non-charitable, if they did so.

Far from heeding such thoughts, however, subsequent case law has tightened still further the restrictions on political activities. In 1949, Mr Justice Vaisey (as he was then) ruled that to defend the existing law was no less political than to promote legislative change; and that even to seek, not necessarily particular legislation but a particular line of administration or policy, is political and so not charitable.[8]

In the same year, the Master of the Rolls, Lord Greene, ruled that the appeasement of racial feeling is a political purpose and not charitable[9] and on that basis the promotion of racial harmony is now held not to qualify for charitable status. Already in 1931, the

High Court had held that a trust to promote a closer and more sympathetic understanding between the English and Swedish peoples was not charitable because it 'was a trust to promote an attitude of mind, a view of one nation by another';[10] and in 1962 the court extended this to exclude any trust 'to promote and aid the improvement of international relations and intercourse'.[11] Finally, in 1981 Mr Justice Slade held that the elimination of injustice was political and hence not charitable[12] with the implication that most activity to promote human rights would not be charitable. Furthermore, he held that seeking a change in the law or in public administration was not a charitable purpose if undertaken abroad instead of in England.

To sum up: the promotion of peace, of racial harmony or of human rights, and the seeking or opposing of any change in the law or in administrative practice, are all political purposes and not charitable. In addition, a number of decided cases have established that the advancement of party politics or of a political doctrine (such as socialism or capitalism) is not charitable.

But this does not mean that a charity cannot seek changes in the law or in administration or even to advance human rights. It can – provided that it does so as a *means* to a non-political end; and provided that end is a charitable purpose and among those purposes specified by the charity's trust deed. So, for example, Age Concern is not prohibited from campaigning for changes in the law that would improve old people's welfare.

USURPING THE FUNCTIONS OF PARLIAMENT?

It is not entirely obvious why twentieth-century judges should have felt compelled to exclude political objects from the ranks of charitable purposes. Lord Parker's reasoning – that the courts are unable to judge whether changes in the law would be for the public benefit – is questioned even in the textbooks.[13] The other main argument used by the courts – that to validate 'law reform' trusts would be to usurp the functions of the legislature[14] is scarcely more convincing.

Apart from anything else, granting charitable status to such trusts is not at all the same thing as actually granting the reforms they seek. There is no guarantee that they will be successful; and if they are, it will be because they have convinced public opinion and Parliament of the need for reform, not because the judiciary has usurped the prerogative of Parliament. Indeed, if never to usurp law-making functions is the rationale, and granted that Parliament had tolerated 'political' charities throughout the nineteenth century, what basis had the courts, from 1917 onwards, for introducing the essentially unprecedented doctrine that political objects could not be charitable?

In any case, political activity by charities often complements rather than competes with Parliament. For as Sir James Jones, then Permanent Secretary at the Department of the Environment, told the Goodman Committee in 1975:

> In the formulation of departmental policy we are very considerably influenced, both at ministerial and at official level, by the views of charitable organisations ... I would not wish to claim that we always see eye to eye with these bodies, since they properly see it as part of their function to identify departmental shortcomings. But I think we would always be prepared to admit that our policy thinking would be narrower and poorer in quality without the stimulus arising from our contact with pressure groups of this kind. We would not therefore favour any argument that charities should abjure lobbying and should be made to stick to their more limited role of direct action in providing housing or relieving distress.[15]

In a similar vein, Des Wilson, director of the Campaign for Lead-Free Air and founder-director of Shelter, recently pointed out that many charities can only do a limited amount to help those in need and went on to put the case for political involvement:

> This restriction on charities is wrong for two reasons: first, because it stops them from adequately demonstrating their incapacity to meet the needs of those they care about and thus silences what should be an influential voice for a greater priority for those in need; second, because charities ... work on the ground, day by day, dealing with the disadvantaged, they are the best educated on how existing 'policies, practice and administration' are actually working out.[16]

Nor is this a particularly new or radical perspective. It is thirty years since the Nathan Committee mapped out the changes implemented in the *Charities Act 1960*; yet in its report it stressed that

Some of the most valuable activities of voluntary societies consist in the fact that they are able to stand aside from and criticise state action, or inaction, in the interests of the inarticulate man in the street. This may take the form of helping individuals to know and to obtain their rights. It also consists in a more general activity of collecting data about some point where the shoe seems to pinch or a need remains unmet. The general machinery of democratic agitation, deputations to the Press, questions in the House, conferences and the rest of it, may then be put into operation in order to convince a wider public that action is necessary. This is one of the fundamental arguments for interposing this wealth of voluntary associations between the citizen and public authority, however enlightened or benevolent this latter may be.[17]

As the law stands, most registered charities remain relatively free to pursue such changes in the law (and in administrative policy and practice) as will advance their primary non-political objectives. The real problem areas are racial harmony, peace and human rights.

RACIAL HARMONY

Perhaps the most ironic aspect of the rule that promoting racial harmony is not charitable, is that the precedent for this stems from a case which disallowed a trust to foster better relations between two *white* groups – the English and Afrikaans communities in South Africa.[18] No doubt such a decision seemed sensible enough in 1949 when no judge could have foreseen the consequences of the large-scale immigration of ethnic minorities that was about to begin. Today, however, the public benefit of racial harmony is widely accepted but its promotion remains non-charitable. In practice, the Charity Commissioners have registered a number of charities in this field such as the Institute for Race Relations, various branches of the Community Relations Commission and several Community Relations Councils. But all have carefully worded trusts expressed in terms of the advancement of education and the promotion of recreational facilities.

The problem with this rather artificial solution is that it limits the scope for engaging in political activity as a means to a non-political end; and it is not at all obvious why the promotion of racial harmony should suffer this disability when other fields of charitable activity do not. In short, this is one area where charity law has clearly lagged behind social and demographic change.

PEACE AND INTERNATIONAL UNDERSTANDING

'Blessed are the peacemakers' – but as already mentioned, 'the improvement of international relations' has been ruled not to be a charitable purpose.[19] On the other hand, there is good authority from a case in 1936[20] that the promotion of peace is a valid charitable object. The two precedents are not easy to reconcile but they do not cover identical objectives and as things stand, the promotion of peace, unlike the improvement of international relations, seems to remain charitable.

In the USA, 'a trust to promote peace by disarmament, as well as a trust to promote peace by preparedness for war, is charitable'.[21] The leading case involved a gift to the World Peace Foundation; its purpose was

> Educating the people of all nations to a full knowledge of the waste and destructiveness of war and of preparation for war, its evil effects on present social conditions and on the well-being of future generations and to promote international justice and the brotherhood of man: and generally by every practical means to promote peace and good will among all mankind.

Allowing the gift, the judge held that 'the final establishment of universal peace among all the nations of the earth is manifestly an object of public charity'.[22]

HUMAN RIGHTS

In 1978 the Charity Commission refused to register the Amnesty International Trust. The trustees appealed to the High Court, but in 1981 Mr Justice Slade upheld the Commission's decision.[23] The Amnesty International Trust was set up in 1977 to administer those purposes of Amnesty International that were thought to be charitable. Amnesty International itself seeks to secure, throughout the world, that prisoners of conscience (i.e. persons who are imprisoned because of their political, religious or conscientious beliefs, or their ethnic origin, sex, colour or language) are treated in accordance with the United Nations Universal Declaration of Human Rights. Amnesty does this by working to secure the release of such prisoners by exposing and publicising their plight, mobilising public opinion and applying persuasion and pressure on imprisoning authorities.

Mr Justice Slade held that the trust was not charitable because two of its objects were political. These were (i) attempting to secure the release of prisoners of conscience and (ii) procuring the abolition of torture or inhuman or degrading treatment or punishment. They were political because they could only be achieved, for the most part, by securing a change in the law or the administrative policy or practice of a foreign country. In his conclusion he said that

> Indisputably, laws do exist, both in this country and in many foreign countries, which many reasonable people consider unjust. No less indisputably, laws themselves will from time to time be administered by governmental authorities in a manner which many reasonable people consider unjust, inhuman or degrading. Amnesty . . . is performing a function which many will regard as being of great value to humanity. Fortunately, the laws of this country place very few restrictions on the rights of philanthropic organisations . . . to strive for the remedy of what they regard as instances of injustice whether occurring here or abroad. However . . . the elimination of injustice has not as such ever been held to be a trust purpose which qualifies for the privileges afforded to charities by English Law. I cannot hold it to be a charitable purpose now.

One bitter comment, following this judgement, was that a law which allows a trust for the prevention of cruelty to animals but forbids one seeking to abolish the torture of human beings 'is indisputably a law which *all* reasonable people will consider unjust'. But strictly speaking Mr Justice Slade did not in fact rule that a trust to uphold human rights could not be charitable; he accepted that a trust which directed pressure against individual persons rather than governments could be charitable, as in the old American precedent[24] which established that a trust to persuade *individuals* to set free their slaves was charitable. Nevertheless, his judgement clearly narrowed down the scope for action to defend human rights; and if one follows his arguments to their logical conclusion, a trust to persuade the Government of Mauritania that it should enforce its laws against slavery and free the thousands of its population who remain enslaved, cannot be charitable because 'the court will not have sufficient means of satisfactorily judging, as a matter of evidence, whether the proposed reversal (of policy) would be beneficial to the community in the relevant sense, after all its consequences, local and international, had been taken into account'.[25]

THE POLITICS OF THIRD-WORLD AID

Granted its premises, that logic cannot easily be faulted; for a judge, sitting in London, may well find it difficult to weigh up the advantages and disadvantages of policies and practices in distant lands. But most of those who have experienced at first hand the grinding poverty, misery and degradation common to many third-world countries, would argue that something has gone awry when legal logic requires them to stand aside from human suffering. No-one would dispute that there is a place for traditional relief work; when famine strikes the hungry must be fed. Yet to stop there would be to ignore the fact that most third-world hunger and poverty is not the result of passing calamities but an enduring and endemic problem.

Anything that tries to do more than alleviate immediate suffering will almost always have political implications. As Brian Walker, director of Oxfam, points out, citing the example of a new well in a remote African village, 'all aid is political':

> Clean water to drink, ample water to irrigate crops and water the cattle. A manifestly humanitarian gesture. But political, too – for a well belonging to the people disturbs the balance of power in that village. Whoever owned the watering place hitherto is now disadvantaged. Normally that means the landlord, the money lender or the local political power boss. Sometimes all three in one. If the people have their own water they do not need to work for the landlord or pay him a tithe, or vote for him in the election, or turn a blind eye when he looks lustfully on their daughters. The political power structure has been disturbed – with a measure of justice flowing towards the poor and away from the powerful. Even when multiplied many times over . . . this remains a modest enough gesture, and is neither radical nor revolutionary. Nonetheless, it is a beginning – a threat to the power base of the rich and the powerful and hence profoundly political.[26]

Others make the point that even to concentrate aid on the immediate relief of hunger, sickness and so on, is fundamentally a political decision. Brian Wren, for example, writes that

> Such a choice can make sense – but only if you believe that poverty is caused by e.g. poor climate, or by a cycle of deprivation passing on inadequacy through particular families, or by the ignorance or fecklessness of the poor; and that the basic structures of society cannot or should not be changed, that the many inequalities in world society . . . are inevitable or justified. One may agree or disagree with this view. The point is, however, that it is by no stretch of the imagination 'non-political'. In our own political tradition it is clearly recognised as on the right of the spectrum: conservative with a small 'c'.[27]

In this connection, it is particularly fascinating to observe that while, during the twentieth century, the English judges have gradually developed the doctrine that charity and politics are incompatible, the churches have moved in the opposite direction, rediscovering their roots and the intimate connection between charity and social justice. So, for example, one finds Dr Kenneth Slack, late director of Christian Aid, arguing that people who want to help their neighbour in need 'must accept that from the moment their aid begins to raise the down-trodden to their feet, it will have social and even political implications'.[28]

Likewise, the second Vatican Council of the Roman Catholic Church re-established in the early 1960s the importance of social justice as an integral element in the gospel message; among the Latin American churches this has been summed up in the slogan, 'the Church has to take sides with the poor'[29] and the present Pope has made the defence of human rights a central message in his preaching. The Anglican Church is also, increasingly, taking the side of the poor; in 1980 its General Synod passed a resolution calling on the government to restore its cuts in overseas aid and the Archbishop of Canterbury, Dr Robert Runcie, has been sharply critical of the Government's policies:

> It is hardly encouraging, to say the least, that British development assistance to poor countries should be cut at a rate much heavier than the . . . cuts being required from other Whitehall ministries . . . I fear that we are in danger of

subjugating the international imperative to the domestic imperative; and if that is so, then it may prove to be a very dangerous and foolish mistake.[30]

The Archbishop went on to say that the church had a right to speak on such political and economic affairs on the ground that, as Christians they 'had an obligation to support the cause of the underprivileged, and if they were to be supported then this meant working for economic reform.'. This growing concern for social justice is very widely shared. Recently even that staunchly conservative churchman, Billy Graham, confessed that, 'The more I learn, the less dogmatic I become. I had no real idea that millions of people throughout the world live on the knife-edge of starvation.'[31]

All these churches are charities, and enjoy the financial advantages of charitable status. But if their concern for social justice continues to develop along these lines they would seem to be on course for a major collision with English charity law. So far this has been avoided; and in 1975, the Charity Commission wrote that

> The pursuance of political activities relating to issues of morality and behaviour by religious charities would not in the normal way be objectionable because such issues are an essential concern of religious bodies and therefore it is not likely to be outside the powers of any charity having wide religious objects to engage in such activities.[32]

Quite so; and the corollary would seem to be that, if you want to promote human rights or advocate world peace, your best bet is to start a new religion.

ROLE OF THE CHARITY COMMISSIONERS

The position of the Commissioners is not an enviable one. It is they who have to decide whether to act on public complaints that charities have overstepped the boundaries of permissible political activity. Moreover, it falls to them to make the difficult decisions as to whether or not would-be charities are too political to be granted registration. So it is not surprising that they have tended to adopt a fairly cautious approach. Their first major public statement on the subject came in their annual report for 1969 which set out guidelines for political activities by charities. These were revised and restated in their report for 1981 and both sets of guidelines are reprinted at the end of the present study (see Appendix 3).

In 1947, the courts had made it quite clear that a charity may engage in political activity provided that activity is *ancillary* to the charity's purposes – i.e. a means to a non-political end.[33] Liberally interpreted, this could be taken to mean that any kind of political campaigning is open to a charity provided that it furthers its charitable aims (and does not stray into party politics); so, for example, the National Council for One-Parent Families would be able, on a liberal interpretation, to organise a march down Whitehall calling for better housing for lone parents.

But the Charity Commissioners' guidelines reject so liberal an interpretation of the established precedents, although they admit that 'the law is based on a limited number of decided cases and there is some danger in trying to stretch them to cover all the ground'. The guidelines go beyond the legal precedents in four main areas:

1. They lay great emphasis on the *style* of political activity. So, for example,

> The powers and purposes of a charity should not include power to bring pressure to bear on the Government to adopt, alter, or maintain a particular line of action. It is permissible for a charity, in furtherance of its purposes, to help the Government to reach a decision on a particular issue by providing information and argument, but the emphasis must be on rational persuasion. (1981 Report, paragraph 54)

A 'reasoned memorandum' is permissible but not a public demonstration. It is not at all clear, however, from what decided cases the Commissioners derive this doctrine: none appear to have ruled out 'pressure' or insisted on 'rational persuasion'.

2. They put a very restrictive interpretation on the expression 'ancillary to charitable purposes'. As normally understood, a charity's purposes are not necessarily something it seeks to achieve directly: the World Wildlife Fund, for instance, does not itself conserve endangered species. Yet

> In general, what is ancillary is that which furthers the work of the institution, not something that will procure the

performance of similar work by, for example, the Government of the day. (*Ibid.*)

And having reinterpreted the term 'ancillary' they proceed to go much further than Mr Justice Slade was prepared to go in the Amnesty case:

> Charities, whether they operate in this country or overseas, must avoid:
> (a) Seeking to influence or remedy those causes of poverty which lie in the social, economic and political structures of countries and communities
> (b) Bringing pressure to bear on a government to procure a change in policies or administrative practices (for example, on land reform, the recognition of local trade unions, human rights, etc.)
> (c) Seeking to eliminate social, economic, political or other injustice.
> (*Ibid.*)

Mr Justice Slade by no means ruled out the possibility that a charity might legitimately do any of these things in furtherance of non-political and charitable purposes.

3. The guidelines also put some emphasis on a distinction between 'education' and 'propaganda', holding the second not allowable to charities:

> There is a . . . tendency for those registered charities which have as a subsidiary object the education of the public in the particular aspect of charity with which the organisation is concerned (for instance the need for the relief of poverty in under-developed countries) to overstep the boundary of what might properly be called education and pass outside their declared purposes into the field of propaganda. There is obvious difficulty in determining exactly where this boundary lies but if a charity with general objects, such as the relief of poverty or distress, issues literature urging the government to take a particular course or organises sympathisers to apply pressure for that purpose to their elected representatives, we think it is clear that the boundary has been overstepped. (1969 Report, paragraph 11)

The Commissioners derive their mistrust of propaganda from two cases where judges commented that political propaganda was not charitable.[34] In fact, both these cases were clear instances of *party* political propaganda; and a court would be free to distinguish both from an education of the public which, while steering clear of party politics or sectarian political doctrines, did not refrain entirely from value judgements. The Commissioners could also, of course, make the same distinction.

4. Finally, the guidelines suggest that if campaigning becomes a major part of a charity's activities, it will have strayed beyond what the law allows:

> A charity can only spend its funds on the promotion of public general legislation if in doing so it is exercising a power that is merely ancillary to its charitable purposes. But here again difficulty arises in defining the boundary between what is merely ancillary and what amounts to adopting a new purpose in itself (*Ibid.*, paragraph 14)

Again it is not easy to see why the Commission favours a restrictive interpretation of the decided cases. Oddly enough, the same annual report mentions that the Upper Teesdale Defence Fund – a trust which had at first devoted *all* its resources to political activity – had been accepted for registration. The promoters of the trust, worried by plans to construct a reservoir, had appealed for funds for the preservation of the flora and fauna of Upper Teesdale and used them to oppose (unsuccessfully) a private Act of Parliament.

> On considering the case we come to the conclusion that the evidence showed that the purpose of the fund was the preservation of the flora and fauna of Upper Teesdale which was an undoubtedly charitable purpose. We also concluded that there was no objection to the trustees using the fund, in furtherance of its purposes, in opposing a private bill. (*Ibid.*, paragraph 23)*

The leading authority generally used to support the view that a charity's political activity must not be too 'substantial' is the National Anti-Vivisection Society case. But a careful reading of the Law Lords' judgements does not bear out such a severe

---

*The Commissioners held that opposing a *private* bill is not political but this is doubtful, at least in the Upper Teesdale case: the courts have clearly stated that seeking a change in public administration is a political purpose. Nevertheless on a liberal construction of 'ancillary' their decision was correct, albeit reached for the wrong reasons.

conclusion. Lord Porter, in his dissenting judgement, had held that a purpose was not political unless the *only* way of achieving it was a change in the law. It is often said that the rest of their Lordships disagreed with this in principle; but, in fact, it is quite clear from their judgements that their reason for not allowing charitable status was precisely that they believed that in this particular case a change in the law *was* the only way of achieving the Society's main object:

> The main purpose of the Society is the compulsory abolition of vivisection by Act of Parliament . . . How else can it be supposed that vivisection is to be abolished? . . . It can only be by Act of Parliament.[36]

Read in context, it is also quite clear that Lord Normand had the same point in mind when he said that

> The problem is, therefore, to discover the general purposes of the society and whether they are in the main political or in the main charitable. It is a question of degree of a sort well known to the courts.[37]

That is not at all to say that substantial political activity is forbidden in furtherance of a (charitable) purpose which does not *necessarily* require legislation.

This is not, of course, the interpretation followed in the Charity Commissioners' guidelines; but it is not without authority from the courts. In the Amnesty case, Mr Justice Slade held that

> The main object of the broadly-defined trust contained in clause 2B must in my judgement be regarded as being the procurement·of the reversal of the relevant decisions of governments and governmental authorities in those countries where such authorities have decided to detain prisoners of conscience . . . The procurement of the reversal of such decisions cannot, I think, be regarded merely as one possible method of giving effect to the purposes of clause 2B, any more than in the *National Anti-Vivisection Society* case the alteration of the law could be regarded as merely one method of giving effect to the purpose of abolishing vivisection. On the construction which I place on clause 2B, it is the principal purpose itself.

In short, while a trust which can *only* achieve its objects by a change in the law or in public administration cannot be charitable, there is no obvious precedent for insisting that a charity must make any political activities it may engage in, a minor aspect of its work.

More generally, it is submitted that the Charity Commission's guidelines on political activity represent a markedly restrictive view of how far charities may campaign for changes in laws or in public policy and administration. Some of their guidance does not appear to have any basis in case law at all; and where precedents might be relevant, the Commissioners seem always to have favoured the least liberal construction possible.

A much more robust interpretation of the law is possible and, confronted with these issues, it is not unthinkable that the courts would take a much more liberal line than the Commissioners have felt appropriate. In practice, however, the Commissioners' views have been so little challenged that they have become a species of conventional wisdom which, unless the climate of opinion changes, would probably prevail in the courts. Nevertheless, the guidelines do not as yet have the force of law and need not be obeyed by charities – provided they are willing to run the risk that sooner or later they may incur the sanctions consequent upon a court deciding that after all the guidelines do accurately represent the law.

THE EFFECT ON ESTABLISHED CHARITIES

These sanctions are, however, a major deterrent. For contrary to a very commonly held belief, a charity which became 'too political' would probably not be de-registered. It is not the charity which would have erred but those responsible for it; and so, as the Commissioners' 1981 report makes clear, 'trustees who stray too far into the field of political activity . . . risk being in breach of trust' and consequently, 'risk being held personally liable to repay to the charity the funds spent on such activity'. At worst the trustees could find themselves bankrupted and it would be a courageous board of trustees that would run the gauntlet of such penalties on any major expenditures. Inevitably this inhibits much overt testing of the boundaries and has greatly hampered the development of case law.

In practice, many well-known charities do engage substantially in political activity without, so far, coming to grief. Most of the more prominent 'campaigning' charities were interviewed in the course of preparing the present study; most wished, for fairly obvious reasons, to remain anonymous but some generalisations can be made. Hardly any of those interviewed felt that they were seriously hampered by the present law, at least as currently administered. Many were quick to point out, however, that this is partly because the Charity Commission seems not to take its own guidelines too seriously and, most of the time, turns a blind eye to the fact that they are constantly breached by a good many charities.

The Commission virtually never, it seems, takes action on its own initiative; by and large, it only moves against a charity when it receives a complaint from a member of the public. Even then, the Commission rarely pursues the matter very far and provided that the charity promises to be more careful in future, it rarely hears any more about the incident.

It is also worth recording that many 'campaigning' charities said that the main constraint on their political activities was not the law or the Charity Commissioners but the need to retain credibility and to avoid upsetting their financial supporters. A frequent theme was the need to retain strong links with all political parties; even the most 'progressive' charities stressed that they needed to influence all shades of political opinion, conservatives as well as radicals. Even if there were no restrictions on political activities, few 'campaigning' charities would greatly change their style. For as one leading charity director summed up this self-censoring attitude, 'Image is crucial. Our work is very political but it is always done in a way which won't alienate people.'

There is no doubt, however, that some campaigning objectives are so clearly 'political' in the eyes of the law that they cannot be made subsidiary to charitable purposes. One way of getting round this problem is to split your organisation into two separate bodies – one charitable and the other 'political'. So, for instance, the National Council for Civil Liberties has the linked Cobden Trust, a charity which conducts research into civil rights. Likewise a number of charities have set up linked campaigning bodies which are free to take an overtly political stance. Youthaid, for example, set up the 'Unemployment Unit' and War on Want has established WOW Campaigns. From interviews and other discussions, it seems clear that this can be a satisfactory solution if carefully thought out and carefully managed; but if the initial planning is inadequate there can be serious problems.

In one case, the two organisations had different trustees who gradually came to very different views of what the overall tandem's policy should be. This problem is avoidable but there is a curiously persistent belief that a dual organisational structure must have separate trustees. There is nothing in law that requires this. The Charity Commissioners have made it quite clear that they do not expect it and it is clearly not a particularly effective way to achieve co-ordination of the two bodies. Another pitfall is to underestimate how much political activity is, in fact, permitted to charities and to hive off much more than is actually necessary to the campaigning wing; so losing, for that work, the advantages of charitable status.

Dual organisational structures should not present insurmountable difficulties; after all, many charities have established trading companies without too much difficulty and the principles are much the same. But there is no doubt that good advice and training at the outset is invaluable.

POLITICAL ACTIVITIES AND REGISTRATION

On the whole, established charities seem not to be greatly hampered by the Charity Commission's guidelines – for, once you are in the club, the rules are not very strenuously applied. Where the guidelines do seem to cause real problems is in relation to new applications for registration.

In preparing the present study, a number of examples of this came to light; but nearly all of these disappointed would-be charities asked to remain anonymous as they did not wish to jeopardise their chances of re-application. It is difficult to discuss such cases since to do so generally requires a description of the bodies' objects, as stated in their governing instruments, and this would not be compatible with preserving their anonymity. In some cases, however, this is not necessary.

Take, for instance, a local youth organisation which applied for registration in May 1981. No answer was received until November when a member of the Commissioners' staff wrote that

> I must apologise for not having been able to reply earlier but this has not been possible due to the volume of work on hand at the present time.

The activities of the Committee appear in the main to be of a charitable nature; however I wouldn't like to see them acting as a pressure group by bringing pressure to bear on the local authorities over various issues as this would be a non-charitable activity and to be acceptable as a charity the activities must be of an exclusively charitable nature. I would therefore like confirmation that activities of this nature will not take place.

The organisation was not prepared to give such an undertaking and decided not to proceed with its application. It is difficult to know how many applicants are turned away by this sort of treatment since the Commissioners do not publish any figures on would-be charities which do not make a formal application for registration. But clearly this is an example where the guidelines have deterred an applicant which, on the face of it, has a perfectly good case for registration. What seems to have been happening is that organisations which probably would not encounter any problems with the law if they were registered charities, have been excluded at a rather tightly guarded door.

There are signs that the double standard this implies is being softened and that the Commission is liberalising its admission policy. The Community Association mentioned earlier, which had campaigned for a pedestrian crossing, has recently been registered as a charity. Nevertheless, until and unless the Commission reconsiders its guidelines on political activity it is doubtful whether the double standard could be abandoned altogether. Unless that is, the Commission decided on a strict application of its guidelines to all established charities; but that seems most unlikely, given the storm it would provoke.

8. Rusty Curbs?

> Falstaff. *But I prithee, sweet wag,*
> *shall there be gallows standing in*
> *England when thou art king, and*
> *resolution thus fobbed off as it is*
> *with the rusty curb of old father*
> *antick the law? Do not thou, when*
> *thou art king, hang a thief?*
> Prince. *No; thou shalt.*
> Falstaff. *Shall I? O rare! By the*
> *Lord, I'll be a brave judge.*
> Prince. *Thou judgest false already;*
> *I mean, thou shalt have the hanging*
> *of thieves and so become a rare*
> *hangman.*
> Falstaff. *Well, Hal, well; and in*
> *some sort it jumps with my humour as*
> *well as waiting in the court, I can*
> *tell you.*
> Prince. *For obtaining of suits?*
> Falstaff. *Yea, for obtaining of suits,*
> *whereof the hangman hath no lean*
> *wardrobe. 'Sblood I am as melancholy*
> *as a gib cat, or a lugged bear.*
> Prince. *Or an old lion, or a lover's lute.*
> Falstaff. *Yea, or the drone of a*
> *Lincolnshire bagpipe.*
> Prince. *What sayest thou to a hare, or*
> *the melancholy of Moorditch?*
> Falstaff. *Thou hast the most*
> *unsavoury similes . . .*

(Henry IV, Pt I)[1]

Given that charities enjoy substantial tax concessions and other privileges, the case for at least some rules and restrictions is hard to resist. Such wide exemptions from taxation are tempting territory for a variety of tax-avoidance schemes and there are various other potential abuses – commerce masquerading as charity, rest homes for weary millionaires, and other pseudo-charities, not to mention fraudulent fund-raising and other forms of outright criminality. Some attempt to sort out the sheep from the goats – to police the boundaries of philanthropy – must be made. The main responsibility for the control of such abuses, as well as the more general regulation of charitable activity, lies with both the Charity Commissioners and the Inland Revenue, supervised by the courts.

THE CHARITY COMMISSION

The Charity Commissioners have, of course, a wider role than this. As the *Charities Act 1960* defines it:

> The Commissioners shall . . . have the general function of promoting the effective use of charitable resources by encouraging the development of better methods of administration, by giving charity trustees information or advice on any matter affecting the charity and by investigating and checking abuses.

They themselves have been anxious to point out that

> The Commissioners regard themselves as the friends and advisers of trustees and a large part of the work of the Commission consists in giving advice to trustees, their advisers and employees.[2]

and even those who are profoundly critical of their role generally pay tribute to their unfailing courtesy and helpfulness.

The Charity Commission was first set up in 1853 in response to long-standing public concern at how the courts' great expense and endless delays made it almost impossible to tackle the neglect and misapplication of many ancient endowments.[3] For the next hundred years the Commissioners' remit was more or less confined to *endowed charities*; it was not until the *Charities Act 1960* (and then almost as an afterthought) that they acquired any real responsibility for the regulation of *'collecting' charities* – those which rely on grants, subscriptions and donations rather than the income from a capital endowment. Even today, a large part of the Commission's work is devoted to assisting and regulating permanent endowments.

The Commission's work takes various forms. In particular, trustees are forbidden in law to alter the primary purposes of their charity (unless the governing instrument specifically allows them to do so); but where these have become out-of-date or otherwise inappropriate, the Commissioners share the power of the court to make a *'scheme'*, validating changes in the charities' purposes. Again, it may be necessary to appoint a new body of trustees or widen their powers of investment. Even where no permanent change is required, the trustees may wish to take some sensible action which is clearly outside their powers and the Commissioners have the authority to issue an order allowing this. Orders are also made to authorise the sale, leasing or mortgaging of land representing permanent endowment or which has been occupied for the purposes of the charity, since such transactions require the Commissioners' *consent* to be valid.

This area of work is carried out by five separate Charities Divisions and two Consent Divisions; their 101 staff make up about two-fifths (42 per cent) of the Commissioners' 238 'front-line staff'.* In 1981, they made some 962 schemes and issued 3,973 orders.

The work of the Official Custodian is another major area of activity. Because charitable lands and other property can often only be vested in individual trustees, charities may often be put to considerable expense when trusts change (e.g. conveyancing charges). But this can be avoided by vesting property in the Official Custodian, who being a 'Corporation Sole', can hold it permanently even though the official holding the post will change regularly. Where the property is stocks or shares, he collects the dividends and remits them free of tax to the trustees. He also deals with applications to participate in the Charities Official Investment Fund – a unit trust scheme established by the Commissioners in 1962. The Official Custodian's 75 staff account for a further 32 per cent of the Commissioners' 'front-line' employees.

The third main area of activity is undertaken by the two Registration Divisions, one in London and the other in Liverpool. Before 1960 there was no registration system; whether or not a body was a charity was purely a question of whether its primary purposes (as specified in its governing instrument) were charitable. Strictly speaking, this has not changed – it is not

---

*Besides the 'front-line' divisions there are some 92 'support' staff. Most of these (73) work in the Establishment Division (personnel management, estimates, office services etc.) but there is also the eight-person Legal Consultants' Division (providing legal advice within the Commission) and eleven staff working in General Division, responsible for policy, public legislation and Parliamentary matters, publicity, inquiries and investigations.

registration, as such, which confers charitable status but the adoption of a suitable constitution. Nevertheless, many charities are legally required to register and most find it expedient to do so; in 1981 some 3,495 bodies were registered. The Registration Divisions are also responsible for obtaining and scrutinising charities' financial accounts. Their 62 staff represent just over a quarter (26 per cent) of the Commissioners' 'front-line' employees.

The Commission makes no charge for any of these services and in 1981 its work cost the taxpayer approximately £4 million. The breakdown of this total among 'front-line' activities is as follows ('support staff' costs are apportioned to the other divisions):[4]

1. Schemes, orders, consents and general advice to trustees . . . . £1.7 million
   (Charities Divisions, £1.1m;
   Consents Division, £0.6m)
2. Official Custodian . . . . £1.2 million
3. Registration . . . . £1.1 million

Much of the work under the first heading is concerned with endowments, which also account for a substantial part of the work of the Official Custodian; and even under the third heading – registration – a fair proportion of the work has to do with endowed charities. In short, although the *Charities Act 1960* extended the Commission's remit to 'collecting charities', at least half of its day-to-day work (and possibly rather more) continues the older tradition of supervising permanent endowments.

Although the volume of work has increased, the Commission, in common with most other government departments, has suffered staffing cuts in recent years and the following table shows how these have been distributed:

	Staffing		Increase/
	1975	1982	Decrease
1. Schemes, orders etc.	108	101	–6%
2. Official Custodian	66	75	+14%
3. Registration	72	62	–14%
4. 'Support' Divisions	108½	92	–15%
All activities	359½	330	–8%

It is clear that the balance of resources has, if anything shifted *towards* the areas of work concerned with endowed charities.

The continuing emphasis and relative protection from staff cuts of the Commission's traditional preoccupations is understandable in the circumstances; the mandatory duties laid on the Commissioners by the 1960 Act require that this part of their work be maintained. But the issue of the Commission's overall staffing levels is an important one. Even in 1975, when it had 9 per cent more staff than today, Bryan Woods, Clerk to the Trustees of the City Parochial Foundation, observed that

> Throughout the history of the Foundation there has been an exceptionally close, friendly and trusting relationship between the Foundation and the Charity Commissioners. If I were to enter a caveat it would be that there is sometimes and of late unacceptable delay in dealing with routine business. On enquiry of the officials responsible the cause is always either a lack of staff or untrained staff because of too rapid a turnover.[5]

Today, it seems that to wait a couple of months even for a reply to a letter, is not an uncommon experience. To register a new charity can take six months or even more which can cause enormous frustration where a project is waiting to get started.

THE INLAND REVENUE

The Charities Division of Inland Revenue's Claims Branch (located in Bootle, Merseyside) plays a rather different role. The Revenue is always keen to stress that its job is not policing charities but collecting taxes; nor does it see its duty as being to raise the absolute maximum possible amount of money in revenue:

> It would be wholly wrong for us – and we do not – pursue forlorn cases or seek to be obstructive. This is not our function. Equally it is not our function to try to substitute our judgement for that of Parliament and to grant relief to bodies, however desirable they may be, which do not come within the law as laid down. Our function is to administer an Act.[6]

Although subsequent measures have added to and refined the reliefs available to charities, the key legislative provision remains the *Income and Corporation Tax Act 1970*, which restated previous legislation. Section 360 spells out the basis on which tax concessions are available and in effect specifies a double test:

> Firstly, is the institution seeking relief *established* for exclusively charitable purposes? Registration with the Charity Commission is conclusive evidence of this but it is not necessarily essential.
> Secondly, has the income on which relief is sought been *applied* to charitable purposes? Registration is irrelevant here; a registered charity will not gain relief on any income that has not been applied to charitable purposes.

Hence the chief task of the Revenue's Charities Division is to decide how far (taxable) income has been applied to charitable purposes. A charity refused relief may appeal to the Revenue's Board of Commissioners (which does not involve any avoidable legal costs) and beyond them to the courts. But obviously the Revenue also has a major interest in what bodies are registered as charities and, wherever there is any room for doubt, they are routinely consulted by the Charity Commission. The Revenue sometimes lodges objections to registration and occasionally appeals to the courts against a decision by the Charity Commissioners, usually only where the decision sets a precedent which would mean a significant loss of revenue.

But the Charity Commission has no standing in the narrower question of whether, for tax purposes, an established charity has applied all its income to charitable objects. The basic point, which is often misunderstood, is that to gain tax concessions it is not enough just to be a charity – in addition, funds must be applied charitably.

The Revenue's Charities Division has a staff of about 150. Most of them work in two large sections devoted to routine tax repayments; one deals with covenants, the other with all other reliefs. In addition, there are two small sections, each of about eight staff. One reviews putative charities' governing instruments to check whether they are, in fact, charities; the other scrutinises financial accounts to check how far income has actually been applied to charitable purposes.

The Revenue, although the most important, is not the only body concerned with fiscal reliefs to charities. Local rating authorities have similar powers and duties with respect to rate relief and apply similar tests; there are also certain minor VAT concessions which involve Customs and Excise on a similar basis.

For many purposes, the overall system of regulation works reasonably well. Nevertheless, there are some areas where problems seem to occur and others where some people argue that attempts should be made to impose greater controls. The field is a difficult and complex one; but a brief review of some of the more contentious issues may be helpful.

MODERNISATION

There is scope under present law to modernise trusts whose purposes have become out-of-date or otherwise inappropriate. The extent to which this is possible is governed by the *cy-près* doctrine:

> Where a clear charitable intention is expressed, it will not be permitted to fail because the mode, as specified, cannot be executed, but the law will substitute another mode, *cy-près*, that is, as near as possible to the mode specified by the donor.[7]

The *cy-près* doctrine often gives satisfactory results and was, in days gone by, regarded as one of the privileges of charitable trusts; for without it a fair number would fail. But the doctrine insists on the change being *as near as possible* and this strict adherence to the donor's wishes does not always yield the most socially useful result.

Take, for example, a case described by Lord Allen:

> I happen to be concerned with a charity in my local village which dates from a bequest made before the first war to set up an isolation hospital in the village. There is now no need for an isolation hospital and anyway this is a need met by the National Health Service. What does one do with the money? . . . The great need of my village is to provide more accommodation for old people. The trustees of this charity would very much like to use the money to do just this, but the Charity Commission pointed out, very properly, that the original bequest for the isolation hospital meant that the hospital was open to people of all ages in the village and that to substitute now a use which limited the use of the money to old people was inconsistent with the original purposes of the donor, whereas we know that if the donor were still alive he would be the first to say that the money should be used

for old people. This is the sort of use that I should like to see made, but I do not see how the Charity Commission could possibly agree to that under the present law.[8]

A similar example has been described by R. D. Woodall. In this case a group of almshouses were no longer required for 'needy widows' and the trustees had allowed them to be used as

> Parish Rooms, where church organisations could meet and where local societies, unable to meet the ever-increasing charges being made by the Education Authority for school accommodation, could assemble on payment of charges which covered heating and lighting. A band of volunteers, guided by experienced craftsmen, rehabilitated the buildings. They have been in constant use, even in school holidays for play groups. A luncheon club has also used the premises ... The Parish Rooms in the almshouses had become a necessity to the community. The Charity Commissioners, however, have correctly realised that the buildings were not being used for the purpose for which they were originally intended and have ruled that the buildings be sold to the highest bidder.
>
> Now, because the law has to be observed, we shall probably lose our Parish Rooms and the land could end as a site for another luxury bungalow ... The subscribers to the building of the almshouses are all in the grave-yard. In my view, however, they would prefer to see the buildings they built continue to serve the community even if it is in a different way from what they envisaged.[9]

The Nathan Committee favoured a relaxation of the *cy-près* doctrine to allow this kind of change, arguing that the 'interest of the locality' should, in suitable cases, be allowed to override a strict interpretation of the donor's intentions. But the *Charities Act 1960*, while it followed the Nathan Committee's prescriptions in most other respects did not implement this recommendation.

The most common counter-argument is that donors would become less willing to make bequests if they felt their wishes might subsequently become completely ignored. There is, in fact, little solid evidence for the claim that a relaxation of the *cy-près* doctrine would dry up the flow of bequests and a more likely result is that donors would spell out much more clearly what they favoured and what they did not; and resort to 'gift-overs' to other charities if they did not wish to allow substantial modifications.

Closely related to the broad question of the *cy-près* doctrine is the abiding problem of a mass of tiny, ancient endowments which benefit a local parish in theory but are no longer of much utility in practice. It was hoped that the 1960 Act would provide the basis for 'local reviews' which would lead to wholesale amalgamations and a better application of resources. But the enthusiasm of the early 1960s soon gave way to disillusionment and it is generally agreed that the results have not been as fruitful as they might have been. In 1981 a Private Member's *Parochial Charities (Neighbourhood Trusts) Bill* was presented to Parliament: 'To provide for the better use of parochial charities for the poor by their amalgamation into neighbourhood trusts.' The Bill would require county councils to propose groupings of parishes or townships whose charities can be merged to form a 'neighbourhood trust' for the larger area. The Charity Commissioners would make schemes to implement the proposals. Income of the trusts would be used to help anyone 'in need, hardship or distress' regardless of the limitations imposed by the original trusts.

The Bill failed for lack of Parliamentary time but is likely to be re-presented.

REGISTRATION

Several aspects of the central registration system administered by the Charity Commissioners have already been considered. Chapters 6 and 7 have looked at the tendency to adopt a relatively narrow interpretation of judicial precedent when considering applications. And the inordinate delays faced by some applicants have also been discussed. Two other issues also deserve a mention.

Not all charities are obliged to register; some – universities, for instance – are specifically exempted. But more generally, no body need register if it has neither any permanent endowment, nor any investment income over £15, nor the use and occupation of any land. This leaves some considerable loopholes. A charity might be set up to collect money for, say, leukemia research and might collect thousands of pounds including covenanted gifts; yet if the money was not invested but simply passed on to some other body, the charity need not register. Many such bodies are undoubtedly honest and well intentioned but the situation does also leave a great deal of scope for malpractice. A rather different kind of example has been described by J. D. Livingston-Booth (late Director of the Charities Aid Foundation):

> Any Company can establish a Foundation, avoid giving it property by allowing it to operate on the Company's premises, avoid it having an Endowment income by funding it by a deed of covenant to be fully disbursed each year. Thereafter the charity is not required under current legislation to register and may long remain unknown to the Charity Commission and to the public. It is very difficult to obtain information about such operations but over thirty Foundations falling into this category have been brought to my notice.[10]

If it was thought worthwhile to close this loophole, it would be necessary to avoid catching a host of very small charities. The principle of the £15 threshold might need to be extended to charities with any kind of income; but clearly £15 would be too low. In 1960, of course, £15 was worth rather more than today – around £100 at 1982 prices. But even £100 is a fairly low income for a charity and a realistic figure might need to be higher still.

The other issue concerning registration is that in Scotland and Northern Ireland there is no central register.* Those who have encountered difficulties with the system in England and Wales might think this is a preferable state of affairs but there have been moves, in both countries, to press for the introduction of registration.

In Scotland the subject was examined by a working party set up by the Scottish Council of Social Service under the chairmanship of Professor A. W. Bradley. In 1972, the *Bradley Report*, having considered but rejected the setting up of a Scottish Charity Commission, recommended the establishment of a Registrar of Charities.[11] Although no government has yet been prepared to legislate for this, the Law Society of Scotland recently revived the matter by issuing a draft Bill for establishing a Register. The Law Society saw the work being undertaken by the Scottish Registrar of Companies.

The *Charities Act (Northern Ireland) Act 1964* closely paralleled the English Act of 1960 but it did not include central registration. This was because the *Newark Report* on which the Northern Ireland Act was based, rejected the idea:

> Some of us were at first inclined to recommend a proper and complete system of registration of charitable trusts . . .

---

*A brief account of charity law and its administration in these two countries is set out in Appendix 1

> But some witnesses who gave evidence before us expressed the fear that a proper system of registration would involve a mass of paper work superintended by a host of officials, and other witnesses were of the opinion that those whose generous instincts led them to give their money or their time to charitable work might be affronted by what was regarded as an unwarrantable piece of interference by the State. Accordingly after full consideration we have decided not to make any proposals relating to the recording of charitable trusts.[12]

Today this decision seems to be regretted. In practice, charities seeking relief from taxation require an exemption certificate from the Inland Revenue. The view seems to be taken that a consistent and rational discussion about the objects of charities is hard to sustain with Inland Revenue, so that the situation is not entirely satisfactory. A further problem is that while rate relief is more generous in Northern Ireland than elsewhere, the rating authorities do not feel themselves obliged to accept that an Inland Revenue exemption certificate is evidence of charitable status. In 1978 the Northern Ireland Council for Social Service put forward proposals to the government for the establishment of a register which were received sympathetically. But the 1979 general election came before anything was done and the present government has decided against a register.

In neither country does it appear to be widely recognised that the Revenue and other authorities administering fiscal reliefs apply a *double* test to bodies applying for relief; so that even if registration provided conclusive evidence of charitable *status* it would still be necessary to show that funds were being *applied* or buildings *used* for charitable purposes. But it is true that a registration system would mean that the first test would become a single hurdle rather than one to be repeated with each fiscal authority. It is worth noting, however, that the same result could be achieved more cheaply by legislating that a Revenue exemption certificate was conclusive evidence of charitable status.

A RIGHT OF APPEAL?

To return to England and Wales. No decision by the Charity Commissioners is final; whether it be a refusal to register, or to allow a particular 'scheme' or any other decision, the applicant always has a right to appeal to the High Court and beyond. In practice this happens very rarely, particularly over registration. Few voluntary organisations, even if they can afford to pay the thousands of pounds necessary to go to court, are willing to divert funds from their more immediate tasks. The need for some form of legal aid is one issue where all parties – the Charity Commissioners, charities, lawyers – are in agreement. Without such cases the law cannot readily adjust to changing circumstances. The courts are capable, by subtle distinctions, of overcoming unhelpful precedents whereas the Charity Commissioners do not allow themselves this freedom though it could be argued that they might go rather further down this path than they have been willing to go in the past.

There is some scope for appeals even without recourse to the courts. Disappointed applicants may always appeal to the Commissioners sitting as a Board if they are unwilling to accept decisions made by the Commission staff. But it has to be said that the existence of this opportunity is not very well advertised. Letters, for instance, informing would-be charities that their trust deeds would not be accepted for registration seem rarely to mention the possibility.

There is a similar opportunity to appeal against Inland Revenue decisions. In addition, the Revenue, unlike the Charity Commission, is able to pay the defendant's costs when it brings a court action. This is only done, however, where a major point of law arises, which affects a whole category of charities or non-charities. Nor will the Revenue pursue such a point unless there is a substantial amount of revenue at stake. So where – as in the majority of cases – the potential tax take is small, the Revenue will simply concede the point. In short the Revenue cannot be expected to pay for test cases except in a narrow range of cases.

ACCOUNTABILITY

Although the Revenue does not see itself as policing charity, its duty to grant relief only on income applied to charitable purposes does effectively check a wide range of possible abuses and misapplications of funds; and because the Revenue brings wide experience and sophisticated techniques to this task, it appears to discharge it fairly effectively. It should not be thought, however, that this provides any comprehensive control of potential misuse of charitable funds. The Revenue is only concerned with *taxable* income and by no means all charity income is taxable. It has no jurisdiction, for example, over money from street or house-to-house collections since such gifts are not liable to taxation. More importantly, when it does discover that a charity's funds have been applied to non-charitable purposes its role is merely to withhold tax relief, not to compel the trustees to stop applying funds in such ways. In short, while the Revenue provides what seems reasonably effective control over tax concessions, it does little to ensure that the bulk of a charity's income is suitably spent.

This latter role falls to the Charity Commissioners, who are entitled, under the 1960 Act, to require any charity to supply them with copies of its financial accounts; they may also order an audit of the accounts of any charity. Moreover any charity having a permanent endowment must submit accounts annually unless specifically exempted from doing so. Such accounts as the Charity Commissioners hold are open to public inspection so that, in principle, no charity's accounts are secret.

It is not easy to see the logic of these provisions. Large collecting charities with an income of hundreds of thousands of pounds or more need not submit accounts so that unless the Commissioners require them, the public have no right to inspect them; yet endowed charities – even those with incomes as low as five or ten pounds – must submit their accounts annually. In any case, the Commissioners seem not to set a high priority to scrutinising accounts:

> When the Commission's office was reorganised after the coming into effect of the Act of 1960, it was intended that there should be regular inspection of the accounts which charities send to the Commissioners under section 8(1) of the Act. It was thought that, as the initial rush of registrations of existing charities died down, some of the staff engaged on that work could undertake this task. The inspection of accounts was duly stated but it never proved possible to carry it out on the expected scale, for a number of reasons. The work of registration and of keeping the register up to date continued to be heavy, while Government policy prevented the recruitment of more staff. Other work had to be given priority and, in particular, the move of part of the Commissioners' office to Liverpool in 1970 caused considerable disruption. . . It was none the less the Commissioners' intention to resume the periodic inspection of accounts as soon as possible. This they were

able to do to a limited extent in 1972, giving priority to the accounts of newly-founded charities, charities whose trusts are expressed in very general terms, charities which it has been decided should be kept under scrutiny for special reasons and some other charities.[13]

This relative lack of priority is also partly because in the Commissioners' view, scrutinising accounts is not a particularly effective way of discovering misapplication of funds:

> Many of the enquiries which are made by the Commissioners arise from complaints which are made to them by members of the public, by individual trustees or employees of charities, by other charities, the police or other sources... From our experience, evidence that something is wrong in the running of a charity is much more likely to be discovered as a result of a complaint than from the study of a charity's accounts.[14]

This may well be so – it is not, after all, very hard to 'cook' accounts so as to hide all trace of malpractice. If control of abuse is the main objective, other more searching investigations may be more appropriate.

But the issue of accountability is not merely a question of controlling malpractice. There is also the much wider question of *public* accountability and the public's right to know how public funds are being spent. For charitable funds are public money, as the Commissioners' Annual Report for 1970 makes clear:

> Our attention has been drawn from time to time to a small minority of Charities which seem to consider that they are entitled to work in secrecy in administering their funds and which are unwilling to disclose, even to responsible enquirers, any information about the way in which they use their income or the nature of the institutions or other beneficiaries to which they make grants... In law, however, all Charitable trusts are public trusts. Once the founder of a Charity has executed a deed or other instrument making a Charitable settlement the property so settled ceases to be his private property and its administration becomes a matter of public concern.

Yet although all charities are required by the Act of 1960 to keep annual accounts, the public has no right to see them unless they are held by the Commissioners.

THE USA EXPERIENCE

As things are, some charities may prefer to preserve this secrecy. But in the longer term this could prove counter-productive. In America, a series of Congressional investigations in the 1950s and 1960s revealed widespread abuse of charitable privileges.[15] In 1965, the US Treasury proposed reforms to prohibit self-dealing (business between a benefactor and his foundation); to require foundations to distribute not only their net income but also a minimum proportion of their assets; to limit themselves to owning 20 per cent of any business corporation and to dilute a donor's control after twenty-five years of his foundation's existence by requiring that he and his relations comprise not more than one quarter of the trustees. These reforms were somewhat unwisely resisted by the charitable world which eventually found itself subjected to the much more draconian provisions of the *Tax Reform Act 1969*. For it is generally accepted in the USA that while the 1969 Act has significantly reduced abuses, it has also had a damaging effect on genuine philanthropy, increasing foundation's administrative costs and greatly reducing the birth-rate of new foundations.

It is often said that the level of abuse in Britain is comparatively low but this not much more than assertion and to those familiar with the USA experience, probably somewhat naive. Many British charities have stories to tell about approaches made to them by people seeking tax avoidance deals and that must be only the tip of the iceberg since it excludes all cases where a charity is deliberately established for legal but dubious purposes. Moves towards greater *public* accountability and support for relatively gentle controls might help to avoid the danger that a determined exposé of dubious charities would provoke unduly harsh legislation at some point in the future.

CHARITABLE GRANTS TO NON-CHARITIES

An issue frequently raised by organisations consulted during the preparation of this study involves the difficulties that can occur when a grant-making trust or other charity wishes to give funds to support the work of a non-charitable body. There is no general legal barrier to this provided the grant is to be applied to charitable purposes. But there are various practical problems. As the Gulbenkian Foundation recently wrote:

> Our other worry in grant giving is the problem of charitable status, long-standing but in the circumstances of increasing need in many areas, a matter of growing concern. For reasons of tax exemption it is the practice of foundations and trusts in the United Kingdom to restrict their giving to enterprises possessing charitable status. This often makes for difficulty when the enterprises happen to operate in areas of community work, inner city deprivation, un-employment and so on which the Foundation has made its particular concern. Enterprises of this kind often do not have charitable status and, under present regulations, cannot get it. Or some get it while others do not. The processes of getting charitable status seem not only inconsistent in decision but often excessively prolonged in negotiation. This impedes good work on the ground as well as the processes of grant-giving which can help with that work.[16]

Some foundations are unable to make grants to non-charities because their trust deeds restrict them to helping only other charities. But in many cases it is merely that the trust has adopted a policy of only giving to registered charities.

This is often said to be because such grants are rarely questioned by the Inland Revenue whereas other grants sometimes become the subject of lengthy correspondence. One solution often adopted is to pass the grant through a third charity and this may be satisfactory where the third party is in a better position to justify the grant (because, for example, it is geographically closer to the non-charity and hence better placed to check it out). But it may merely shift the burden of proof.

From discussions with the Revenue it seems possible that grant-making trusts might be able to take a rather more robust line without encountering as many difficulties as some seem to envisage. Provided that grants are made for specific *charitable* activities and not towards the general expenses of a non-charity, and provided that the grantors supply (with their accounts) a few sentences explaining what activities the grant was made towards, there should not usually be any come-back from the Revenue.

But obviously there will continue to be problems where the charitable status of the activities to be funded is in doubt. To deal with that type of situation may well require time-consuming discussions with the Revenue and it might well be that some intermediary charity which could specialise in such matters might be useful. The Charities Aid Foundation, which is such an intermediary grant-handling trust, currently only makes grants to registered charities but could in principle take on this role. Alternatively, some new body might be created for this purpose.

FROM GAMEKEEPER TO GATE-KEEPER

For the first hundred years or so the role of the Charity Commission could be characterised as that of a 'gamekeeper' – guarding the property and purposes of permanent endowments. The extension of its remit, since 1960, to include 'collecting' charities has added a 'gate-keeper' role – controlling access to tax concessions and grants from foundations. But as was discussed earlier, the provisions of the 1960 Act, together with restrictions on staffing levels, have hampered the development of the 'gate-keeper' function. It is difficult to avoid the overall impression that endowed charities have tended to find the Commission helpful and outgoing, whereas new 'collecting' organisations seeking registration often speak of a more adversarial or even obstructive attitude. It would be wrong to blame the Commissioners for this – many of their mandatory duties relate to endowments and without a substantial increase in staffing levels (or the legislative removal of some of their mandatory duties) it is not reasonable to expect them to get far with developing their work for 'collecting' charities.

Are changes needed? That depends on how seriously one takes the expressions of support made by all recent governments for voluntary organisations. This has not been confined to rhetoric: under successive governments, statutory grants to voluntary organisations have increased in real terms. Most of these organisations are 'collecting' charities rather than the endowed variety and the proposition that there should be more such bodies enjoys all-party support. But more play-groups, more community care schemes, more self-help groups and so on, means more 'collecting' charities and more work for the Charity Commissioners.

In short, two government policies appear to conflict. Support for 'voluntarism' implies enlarging the Charity Commission; restricting public expenditure implies shrinking it. But is the conflict real? Charities bring other resources to bear as well as requiring some public expenditure, and so, in a limited way, contribute to both policies. And the sums in question are not large since the Commission's total budget for staff costs is only £3.3 million.

An alternative approach, much applied elsewhere in recent years, would be for the Commission to charge for its services. The Commissioners do not favour this[17] but if the government were unwilling to increase the Commission's budget, some would see charging as preferable to limping on with inadequate resources. It is interesting, in this connection, that in Scotland, where a charity has to apply to the courts for many of the Commission's services, a 'scheme' will generally cost at least £300 and often more. Much more moderate charges than this could provide the basis for more adequate staffing levels and even allow some of the existing government funding to be diverted to a pilot fund for key appeals to the High Court.

III. An Agenda For Change

9. Time for a New Start?

Laws are like cobwebs, which may catch small flies, but let wasps and hornets break through.

(Johnathan Swift)[1]

The first part of this study – chapters 1 to 4 – traced the concept of charity from its origin as part of a fierce attack on social and economic injustice, through the Tudor and Stuart emphasis on the relief of poverty to its present technical meaning in English law. The next four chapters examined how the current application of this modern conception awards the tax concessions conferred by charitable status to expensive services mainly catering for the well-to-do but denies them to pressure groups; how it tends to lag behind voluntary action in responding to social and economic change; how far its guardians – the courts, the Charity Commissioners and the Inland Revenue – have effectively promoted the fruitful development of the voluntary sector; and certain ways in which the current system tends to impede such development.

A number of problems areas have emerged, although what counts as a problem seems to depend to some extent on who you are. It could be that the present government, for example will remain convinced that the existing approach is 'broadly satisfactory'; and if by that one means that the underlying framework is essentially sound, many might well agree. But if one means that there are no changes which would help the development of voluntary action, then there are more than a few in the churches, in voluntary organisations and in community groups who will beg to differ. And some will go further and advocate a completely new start.

BEYOND CHARITY?

The main advocates of a wholly new approach have been the members of the Charity Law Reform Committee, founded in 1971 by a number of individuals and organisations dismayed by the removal of charitable status from the Humanist Trust. 'Charity law reform' somewhat understates their goal, which is a radical break with tradition abandoning the concept of charity altogether. Instead they have proposed the introduction of a new legal category to include all non-profit-distributing organisations (NPDOs).[2]

All NPDOs would be entitled to every tax concession and other privilege which charities currently enjoy; but they would be free to pursue any purpose of any kind and there would be no restrictions on political activities. The only thing that would be prohibited would be any kind of private benefit and, to ensure that no monies passed into private hands, regulations would be stringently enforced. The existing law of charity would continue alongside the new arrangements but charities would be able to opt for NPDO status. All NPDOs would have to register and pay a significant registration fee which would defray the costs of policing the system. The Committee also suggested that the remit of the Charity Commissioners should be broadened to include supervising NPDOs, a proposal greeted, however, with something less than enthusiasm by the Commissioners themselves.

The Committee saw 'the major defect in the law' as being 'the exclusion of all political activity on the part of a charity'. That is, of course, a considerable exaggeration; for although the extent of freedom is disputed, the law by no means prohibits political activities by charities. But the Committee was concerned to bring tax concessions and other privileges to a much wider range of bodies:

> Among the types of body to benefit from the reform we would expect professional organisations, political parties and law reform organisations to be prominent.[3]

The fundamental idea running through all this is that in a democracy, opinions as to what benefits the public and what does not are bound to differ. Hence the appeal of a system which rejects value-judgements and simply relies on the apparently objective criterion of non-profit-distribution:

> Civil servants would no longer be required, under pretence of administering the law, to make arbitrary decisions involving value judgements about which organisations 'deserved' tax relief or were 'desirable' in the public interest – decisions which are particularly difficult if not impossible and indeed objectionable in a plural society where there is a vigorous public debate about future policy.[4]

WHO WOULD BENEFIT?

The NPDO approach undoubtedly has some attractive features, most of all, perhaps, its comparative simplicity when set alongside the labyrinth of charity law. And if western democracy and political pluralism are worth defending with Tridents and cruise missiles, it is difficult to see why the institutions defended are not worth relatively minor tax concessions, at a tiny fraction of the cost. Certainly other countries – Germany, for instance – have allowed tax concessions of this kind without apparent ill-effect and even in Britain, gifts to political parties are given considerable relief from Capital Transfer Tax. But as with any proposal for major changes in public policy, *all* the effects of introducing the NPDO approach need to be considered.

Two major issues are particularly important: the scope offered for tax avoidance by third parties and the overall balance of benefit. The Charity Law Reform Committee summarily dismissed the first:

> The NPDO might at first sight seem to offer many opportunities for mere tax avoidance. We are satisfied that this is not so: the regulations we propose will prevent the money saved on tax from being got out of the organisation except by criminal evasion.[5]

But others have been less sanguine. The Inland Revenue, in particular, saw considerable scope for abuse:

> There are two particular kinds of abuse which would need to be considered. One is the withdrawal of funds or benefits from the body for the benefit of those who are members of it. With respect, the Charity Law Reform Committee...

have not covered as fully as one may need to, things like benefit in kind: so that members of a golf club or a dining club, did not come within this kind of benefit... One would need a fairly severe and complicated system (of control). There is a second class of problems... Under present law, we have a protection in the case where a charity seeks to use its relief in order to set up a tax avoidance scheme (on which it may get a commission) the main benefit of which goes to a high-rate tax-payer outside. We have a situation where... there is scope... to swap income for capital between the high-rate tax-payer and the charity and in effect to sell the charitable exemption. This is not in our view, an application of money for Charitable purposes. The object of the charity is not to relieve tax for a high-rate tax-payer. Within the scope of the present definition we have successfully tackled devices of that kind... If one took the definition, as such, straight out of Charity Law Reform Committee's paper, this would give us no protection... Somewhere between the two, one must try to construct a compromise. I do not see what that compromise will be or how it can be made to work.[6]

The second major issue concerns the overall balance of benefit. The Committee's proposals could well confer tax-exempt status on a range of bodies such as the Automobile Association (which had an operating surplus of over £4 million in 1981), the Consumers' Association (publishers of *Which*?) and a host of other NPDOs possibly even including BUPA, the St James Clubs and many more whose claim to favourable treatment is not immediately obvious. And they would leave untouched all the existing anomalies discussed in chapter 5 – public schools, private hospitals and so forth.

Such an approach is not impractical; the French system of tax concessions for 'associations' is more or less along these lines. But it is important to note the corollary: a wider definition means a much larger class of organisations and the result, almost inevitably, is that the tax-concession butter is spread much more thinly. The French 'association' gains very much less from its special tax status than charities get in Britain. And even supposing NPDOs gained all the charity concessions initially, it seems probable that as, over time, the structure of taxation changed so the concessions would be eroded.

TAX CONCESSIONS: A RIGHT OR A PRIVILEGE?

Some would welcome that, and argue against the whole principle of tax concessions for charities; for like Gladstone in 1863, they would condemn them as 'a grant of public money without public control'. Surely, they would argue, the £200 million or more that would flow into the Exchequer if concessions were abolished could be better spent than on an undiscriminating subsidy of activities whose contribution to the general public good is very patchy? Better, surely, to abolish all exemptions and direct the proceeds to discretionary grants for those charities able to demonstrate a real public benefit? They would get more and be able to contribute more to the general good while those charities which did not serve a truly public purpose would have to find their own resources.

Others would resist this onslaught. They would point out that relying on government grants instead of tax exemptions means that the definition of what serves the general public good will lie in the hands of the government of the day and that it is obvious that no single government can possibly have a monopoly of insight into what best serves the public interest. The great virtue of the voluntary sector, they would claim, is that it accommodates a wide range of divergent, even conflicting views on what the general good might actually be. Minority views are often proved right in the longer term and the price of protecting them is a willingness to tolerate pluralism. So the modest benefits of tax exemptions should not be sacrificed to the passing prejudices of the particular political party temporarily in power.

Their second major argument would be that the purpose of tax relief on *gifts* to charity is to encourage donors to make gifts they otherwise might not. As a historical explanation this is dubious but it may be true in practice even though the evidence is slim.

Some would go further still and, like Disraeli in 1863, assert that the principle of tax exemption 'is not a privilege – it is a right'. So, for instance, the Independent Schools Joint Committee has trenchantly rejected the view that 'fiscal benefits represent a form of subsidy by the State':

> The income of individuals and corporate bodies belongs to those to whom it accrues. It is for Parliament to decide how much shall be removed in the form of taxation. Freedom from taxation is not a form of subsidy.[7]

The opposite standpoint had been strongly put by the Royal Commission on the Taxation of Profits and Income (the Radcliffe Commission) in 1955:

> Accepting the view that all parts of the national income are prima facie subject to a tax on income, the system does amount in effect to a grant of public moneys towards the furtherance of such causes as come within the legal category of charity.[8]

In the United States, the view that tax concessions represent a form of government spending has been widely accepted; and the concept of a 'tax expenditure', advocated by the economist Stanley Surrey,[9] is now used in the official US budget. This development has not, however, gone unchallenged; such thinking has been strongly criticised by writers such as Irving Kristol:

> In the course of making these arguments, a very interesting rhetorical transformation takes place. They begin to think and talk as if the basic decision to subsidize had already been made – only, the subsidies are now incarnated in the tax system rather than in positive legislation. So they come quickly to refer to all exemptions and allowances in our tax laws as 'tax subsidies' or even 'tax expenditures'. But note what happens when you make this assumption and start using such terms. *You are implicitly asserting that all income covered by the general provisions of the tax laws belongs of right to the government, and that what the government decides, by exemption or qualification, not to collect in taxes constitutes a subsidy.* .. When a man makes a tax-deductible gift to charity, whose money has he given away? Traditionally, it has been thought that he gives away his own money, and that the tax deduction exists only to encourage him to give away his own money for such a purpose. Today, however, one hears it commonly said that he has only in part given away his own money – in actuality, he has also given away some 'public' money... It is then said – indeed, it is now a cliché – that the object of his philanthropy (a museum, say) is '*in effect*' being subsidized by public monies. What we are talking about here is no slight terminological quibble... The conversion of tax incentives into 'tax subsidies', or 'tax expenditures' means that 'in effect' a substantial part of everyone's income really belongs to the government – only the government, when it generously or foolishly refrains from taxing it away, tolerates our possession and use of it.[10]

It is worth noting that Kristol begins this tirade by speaking of a *rhetorical* transformation. For it has to be said that a moment's sober reflection will reveal that the whole debate has more to do with rhetoric than logic. It may be none the worse for that but it should not be allowed to obscure the real issues, since it is patently obvious that a major issue of public policy looms behind the hair-splitting. By all means let us forswear the language of 'subsidy', 'tax expenditures' and the like; but to do so cannot mean that our elected representatives should not, from time to time, consider the effects of tax concessions and decide whether what once made sense remains reasonable as circumstances change.

Indeed, there can be no doubt that neither Parliament as a whole, nor any of the major parties have ever contemplated doing otherwise. The Heath government, when it introduced VAT in 1973, refused to give any general exemption for charities; and the present government, when shifting some of the burden of taxation from income tax to VAT (at considerable cost to charities) refused any major concessions. Likewise the Labour government in 1976 did not initially intend to exempt charities from Development Land Tax and complete exemption did not come until 1981.

So it is quite clear that tax concessions for charities are not a right but a privilege granted by Parliament – a privilege that has to be justified like any other public policy. And once put in those terms, it is obvious that the chief criterion for granting tax concessions must be whether or not they will confer some benefit on the public as a whole or on an appropriate section of the public. That does not imply that Parliament will necessarily wish to adopt the same criteria as those developed by the courts or even rule out the very broad concept of public benefit advocated by the Charity Law Reform Committee. But it does mean that some test of public benefit has to be found and the choice of such a test clearly cannot avoid a value judgement.

PUBLIC BENEFIT REVISITED

The clash of values is the stuff of politics and it is not surprising that views on the best way forward vary greatly. Some favour the NPDO solution; others the 'zero option' of abolishing tax concessions for charities altogether. But there are a number of possibilities in between these two extremes. There are those who would settle for the status quo despite its anomalies. Others, while rejecting the zero option would, with the Radcliffe Commission, nevertheless argue that

> What is amiss in the present system is not the idea of giving. . . tax relief in respect of charity but the undue width of what ranks as a charity for this purpose.[11]

But those who favour a public benefit criterion more stringent than that of the courts, hold differing views on just how stringent the criterion should be. Ben Whitaker, for example, a member of the Goodman Committee, strongly dissented from his fellow members' views about 'costly fees, subscriptions and charges for services'. In his minority report he pointed out that

> The effect of these. . . is to restrict the benefit of some so-called charities (not only schools and hospitals) to those people who are generally already most privileged financially and socially. The fact that this is achieved often at the expense of the poorer taxpayers means that the net result can be a redistribution of advantages from the less well-off to the rich – a concept of charity that did not occur even to Jonathan Swift and requires his pen to do it justice.[12]

He went on to suggest that instead,

> Charitable status should be allowed only to those institutions whose work is intended by its objects directly and primarily (but not exclusively) to be of benefit to the poor, and which do not charge fees. . . at such a level that the effect in practice is to exclude those with average or below average incomes.[13]

Or, as he puts it elsewhere:

> A modern definition of charity should focus primarily on the prevention and relief of deprivation (whether physical mental or social). . . . Religious bodies should be granted charitable status only in so far as they carry out otherwise charitable activities: e.g. for their work in relieving poverty, but not for providing vestments.[14]

Whitaker's views on public benefit are oddly close to the intentions of the charity statute of 1601[15] although he also makes the case for pressure groups being for the public benefit, provided they too concentrate on the needs of the deprived and disadvantaged.

Whitaker's position has had its critics;[16] his doubts about continuing charitable status for expensive private schools and hospitals are fairly widely shared, but the notion that charitable benefits should be largely restricted to the poor probably enjoys less support than the principle that, to qualify as a charity, no institution should exclude the poor or benefit the well-off disproportionately. And, in practice, those who adopt even that more limited principle, confine their proposals to advocating the reform of private education.[17]

Yet even with this relatively narrow focus, problems start to crop up when one considers how the principle might be implemented. The advancement of education, as such, subsumes a wide variety of charitable activity, much wider than schools, let alone private schools, and nobody today seriously advocates eliminating it as a valid charitable purpose (except for those few who favour the zero option of abolishing charities' tax concessions altogether). But a more selective approach would require complex legislation which would not easily avoid causing unintended damage to charities other than those at which it would be aimed – to alternative or experimental schools such as the White Lion Free School, for example, or to those which offer a specialist education such as music or bilingual schools.

A more fundamental problem is that removing charitable status may not merely remove tax concessions: it would undermine the legal basis of some schools altogether. For at law, if a trust is held not to be charitable it cannot simply carry on as a non-charitable, non-profit-distributing purpose trust; its assests must be applied *cy-près* – that is, to the most similar charitable purpose that can be found – and consequently the trustees of some schools would be legally obliged to submit to the Charity Commissioners a scheme for applying their assets to some purpose that remained charitable. In short, removing charitable status from some schools is tantamount to abolishing them. That might not, of course, disconcert all the opponents; but it is certainly a great deal more than simply correcting a tax concession anomaly.

Merely to remove tax concessions from an arbitrarily defined section of charities would encounter considerable opposition, however; for many of them, and by no means merely the more traditional in outlook, would fear that once such a precedent was set, the process would continue to the point where only the most non-controversial of activities remained charitable.

THE 'METAL BOX' APPROACH

'If I were you I would not start from here', as the peasant said to the lost tourist. A less arbitrary approach would begin not from particular charitable *purposes* but from first principles because the fundamental issues have nothing to do with education or with healthcare, as such; but with whether or not there is a genuine benefit to the public.

Indeed, as was argued in chapter 5, it is by no means certain whether charities which mainly or entirely cater for the well-to-do are, in fact, applying their income to charitable purposes. Under existing law, a plausible case could be made that while they are undeniably charities, they are not entitled to tax concessions and rate relief. Whether the courts would uphold such a view, however, is entirely another matter. But if Parliament required them to do so, next to no violence would be done to the structure and logic of the case-law heritage.

And just this approach has, in the past, succeeded in gaining all-party support. In 1975 the House of Commons Expenditure Committee unanimously agreed[18] that

> Legislation should be introduced whereby all Charities should be required to satisfy the test of 'purposes beneficial to the community'.[19]

Critics have pointed out that the existing law already requires exactly that.[20] This is true but trivial – the Expenditure Committee made it amply clear that what they intended was a *stricter* public benefit requirement than is currently applied by the Inland Revenue and rates authorities:

> We believe that our recommendation to make a test of public benefit the overriding consideration. . . accords both with the spirit in which many of our sixteenth century public schools were founded and with a widespread public feeling today that charitable activities today should not be manifestly devoted to privilege or exclusiveness. We would therefore expect that our new test of 'purposes beneficial to the community' would only admit to charitable status those institutions which manifestly devote the education they

provide towards meeting a range of clear educational needs throughout the whole community.[21]

The Committee also made it clear that they were only pointing the way forward, not providing tablets of stone:

> As we are neither lawyers no parliamentary draftsmen we consider it foolhardy to attempt to draft a statutory definition ourselves, but we feel that it should be perfectly possible for experts to do so given the guidelines we now outline.[22]

The real shortcoming of the proposal was that it overlooked the problem of what happens to charities that lose charitable status. But this is not difficult to rectify: the *Metal Box rule* shows that the courts can allow charities to retain charitable status while requiring them to pay taxes and rates and a new public benefit test laid down by legislation could do the same.

The Expenditure Committee was unquestionably correct in considering it foolhardy for non-experts to draft statutory definitions; nevertheless a loosely-drafted fictitious Bill may be useful, by way of illustration, provided it is understood that it would need considerable refinement by lawyers and parliamentary draftsmen:

CHARITIES (TAX CONCESSIONS) BILL

> A BILL to clarify the law relating to the taxation of charities and their exemption from other public levies.
>
> *Whereas* existing practice permits that the income of a charitable trust may be deemed applied to charitable purposes even where the benefits accrue entirely or primarily to the relatively well-to-do, it is the intention of the present legislation to allow this to continue only in a much more limited range of circumstances.
>
> *Wherefore* be it enacted by the Queen's most Excellent Majesty, by and with the advice of the Lords Spiritual and Temporal and Commons, in this present Parliament assembled, and by the authority of the same as follows:-
> 1. For the purposes of awarding tax concessions, and other exemptions from public levies, on income applied to charitable purposes, 'public benefit' shall be deemed to signify only such benefits as are generally accessible or available, or may be used or shared by all members of the community.

2. This does not exclude such benefits as may be extended to the whole community yet are, by their nature, advantageous only to a few. But it shall not be taken to include any form of relief accorded to a selected few out of a larger number equally willing and able to take advantage of it where the basis of selection involves an obligatory fee or subscription greater than 75 per cent of the benefit obtained unless the majority of such fees are met by charitable or other public grants; or unless the fee is less than the ordinary weekly supplementary benefit rate for a person living alone. . . .[23]

THE LOGIC OF TAX CONCESSIONS

If the issue is to be tackled at all, the 'Metal Box approach' has several advantages: it tackles the nub of the problem – public benefit – rather than seeking to tamper with the types of purpose considered charitable; and, by so doing, avoids the danger of unintended damage to innocent bystanders. It avoids the inevitable complications of separate regimes for charitable status and tax exemption. And it offers a choice to an institution caught by its provision – either to modify its policies and practices so as to meet the more stringent criterion of public benefit or to lose the marginal benefits of tax concessions.

But perhaps its chief merit is that it complies with a generally accepted principle of tax relief, that its effect should not be regressive. That principle is supported by every major political party. Sir Geoffrey Howe, for example, arguing the case for private sector involvement in social welfare, stresses that

> As we develop our thinking along these lines we must never cease to proclaim that the objective of such an approach is not to defend a rump of privilege for the few, but to enlarge the bridgehead of choice for the many.[24]

A good example of this principle applied is the present government's refusal to raise the £25,000 ceiling on mortgage interest tax relief. Closer to the present context, it is striking that Dr Rhodes Boyson (Under-Secretary of State for Education and Science) recently defended the Assisted Places scheme on the grounds that it is quite the opposite of regressive:

> I should like to report on an area which has been of much concern to Labour Members. In earlier debates they stated

at some length that the scheme was really intended to help fairly well-off families who would send their children to independent schools anyway. We refuted that view then and I am pleased to report that, in the event, we have been able to achieve what we have always said was the scheme's objective – to help the less well-off. In the first year of the scheme, one-third of the places were awarded entirely free because of the low income of families. Two-thirds of the assisted places went to pupils from families with incomes below the national average. Only 6 per cent of the assisted pupils are from families whose income exceeds one-and-a-half times the national average family income. This is a major achievement. Despite the doubts of Opposition Members, we have shown that with a properly designed scheme it is quite possible to help the less well-off benefit from the education provided at good independent schools.

I have looked at the list of applications. The parents come from all walks of life – shop assistants, bus drivers, agricultural workers, postal workers, nurses, one-parent families and the unemployed. I do not think that the rich – such as Members of Parliament – are included in that list. I am sure that that will win approval from both sides of the House.[25]

If that reasoning were applied to the issues of tax concessions and other reliefs for charities, might it not be that the 'Metal Box approach' would also 'win approval from both sides of the House'? For as we have seen, there was all-party support for the idea in 1975 and, if ideological assumptions were temporarily suspended, there is no obvious reason why a more stringent criterion of public benefit should be politically controversial today.

And it is well to keep a sense of proportion: the issue has more to do with principle and the coherence of charity law than with the survival of charities that primarily benefit the well-to-do. Their fees would only increase marginally if the 'Metal Box approach' were adopted and although one could hardly expect them to volunteer for extra taxation, they might well prefer that minor burden to the catastrophe of losing charitable status altogether.

A DISPASSIONATE POSTSCRIPT

One final point is important. The issue of 'public benefit' has been considered at length because it is central to the law of charity and to the tax concessions charities enjoy. For those charities which rely on public donations rather than fees, and whose benefits go not to the donors but to needy third parties, tax concessions are often crucially important. So any changes in the legal meaning of charity or the basis of tax exemptions may have considerable implications for what they are able to achieve. To that extent they will be anxious that any legislative changes do not have unintended side-effects which harm their work. Hence the importance of identifying ways of reforming 'public benefit' which would not run that risk.

Indeed, for them such reforms are not a priority or an objective at all. It cannot be too strongly emphasised that none of the charities consulted in the course of preparing this study shared any particular enthusiasm for a more stringent public benefit criterion. This is not surprising, of course, for leaving aside any personal views, the voluntary sector generally would be unlikely to profit from any such tightening up. A much more popular cause would be reforms which liberalised other aspects of the law of charity.

10. Piecemeal Reform

It is not what a lawyer tells me I may do; but what humanity, reason, and justice tell me I ought to do. . . . Bad laws are the worst sort of tyranny.

(Edmund Burke)[1]

'Tis not denied, but gladly confessed . . . that great measure of truth which we enjoy. . . . But he who thinks we are to pitch our tent here, and have attained the utmost prospect of reformation . . . that man by this very opinion declares he is yet far short of truth.

(John Milton)[2]

Discussions and interviews with a wide range of charities and other interested parties have revealed substantial support for the general proposition that the law and administrative practice relating to charities could be considerably improved. When it comes to specific change, however, there is less unanimity if only for the obvious reason that the particular difficulties encountered by individual organisations vary according to the nature of their work and circumstances. This is not at all to suggest that broad agreement on what should be done is out of the question; merely that the systematic consultation which would be needed to achieve such a consensus has yet to be undertaken.

This study's purpose is to provide a fresh analysis of the most salient issues and of possible options for change as a prelude to such consultation. This chapter attempts a brief survey of the many possible changes that have been recommended at one time or another. It cannot pretend to be exhaustive nor does it, by and large, consider the broad options examined in the last chapter though it should perhaps be said that there does not seem, at present, any very broad support either for the Charity Law Reform Committee's proposals or for a more stringent interpretation of 'public benefit'. What follows concentrates, instead, on possible piecemeal reform in the middle ground, ordering the issues along the lines of chapters 6-8.

BUILDING A NEW SOCIETY

Chapter 6 identified a wide range of issues which arise because social and economic change has thrown up new attitudes, needs and problems which do not slot easily into the existing framework of charity law. In a few cases, existing court decisions rule out the adoption of certain purposes or activities: advice-giving and the general benefit and welfare of children in care are arguably the most curious examples. In many cases, however, it is not so much the existence of a legal precedent that causes difficulties as the tendency of the Charity Commissioners and the Inland Revenue to extrapolate established judicial reasoning to cover circumstances never actually considered by the courts. Action against unemployment; overseas aid under the fourth Macnaghten head; sport and amateur art; and participative management styles are just four of the areas where the outlook of the gate-keepers seems to lag behind changing perspectives in the voluntary sector and society more generally.

Various ways of lightening the 'dead hand' of precedent have been suggested. The Goodman Committee favoured a new list of charitable purposes to replace those described in the preamble to the statute of 1601. At the end of their report[3] they set out their proposed guidelines and this Goodman post-amble, as it might be described, is set out in Appendix 2. The list is largely a codification of established purposes and does not markedly extend the ambit of charity. The main extensions appear to be the *prevention* of poverty (a); the advancement of ethical and moral teachings – humanism as distinct from religion (k); housing for those in special need (m); sport (o); the welfare of children (p); advice-giving (v); and the removal of all restrictions on overseas aid.

In some respects, however, the Goodman guidelines appear likely to harden existing restrictions and obstruct judicial creativity. So, for example, they enshrine the questionable distinction between education and propaganda (e) which could prove less than helpful. And '(x) the advancement and improvement of the standards of efficiency of industry, commerce and agriculture' is a narrower conception than that so far allowed by the courts and threatens to remove one possible basis on which the courts could permit a broadening of action against unemployment.

A more serious criticism is the vagueness of some of the guidelines. Take '(v) Advice-giving in suitable circumstances', for example; it is far from obvious whose view of what might be 'suitable circumstances' would apply: on a narrow interpretation that kind of advice-giving is already a valid charitable purpose. So, too, the prevention of poverty in 'suitable cases'. Does assistance for 'immigrants' (u) extend to their children born in Britain? And what exactly is '(l) The provision of social welfare services for those in need of them'?

An alternative approach might be to renounce any attempt to provide the courts with a new 'dictionary' of charitable purposes and concentrate on those where problems are actually encountered. This would begin from exploratory discussions with the Charity Commissioners and the Inland Revenue to establish how far there might be scope for a more robust and imaginative view of what the courts might hold if confronted by existing or would-be charities seeking to meet new needs or old needs in new ways. Recently, it should be said, there have been encouraging signs that the Commissioners, in particular, are prepared to adopt a less restrictive outlook; and since most of the difficulties have not arisen from cases actually decided by the courts but from analogy with such cases, such a shift in attitudes could go a very long way indeed to removing a source of considerable grievance.

Nevertheless there will remain certain areas such as advice-giving where the Commissioners are unlikely to feel able to ignore judicial precedent. Dialogue and discussion would establish what these were and they would have to be tackled, if that seemed desirable, in other ways. One possibility would be to pursue test cases in the courts. An interesting experiment of this kind is a test case which will soon be heard on the extent to which the provision of housing is a valid charitable purpose. The trust in question has five purposes some of which are likely to be held non-charitable but the merit of this approach is that it can provide a clear indication of exactly where the courts hold boundaries to lie. Carefully constructed trusts of this kind put first to the Charity Commissioners and the Inland Revenue and subsequently – if these authorities felt unable to accept the validity of some or all of the purposes – to the courts could map out where parliamentary legislation provided the only means of extending the ambit of charity.

The chances are that certain purposes would be held non-charitable even by the courts, though the residue could be much smaller than might appear at first sight. For these, amending legislation, along the lines of the *Recreational Charities Act 1958* would be needed and this might well be an attractive option for a Private Member's Bill. And since social and economic change will continue to throw up changing needs and attitudes it could be that over the years a series of such amending acts would be felt desirable.

POLITICAL ACTIVITY

Chapter 7 examined the question of how far a charity may engage in 'political' activity. Certain boundaries are fairly clearly established: no charity may seek to advance any party political cause or any other politically sectarian purpose; nor may a charity's chief purposes include securing or preventing a change in the law or in administrative policy and practice. It is also clear that in the eyes of the judges to work for peace or racial harmony or human rights is to seek a political purpose. Finally, it is well established that a charity may engage in political activity in furtherance of its primary, non-political purposes.

The grey area is how much and what sort of 'political' activity a charity may undertake as a means to 'non-political' ends. There is little in the way of legal precedent and, as with the issues considered in the previous section, the Charity Commissioners have extrapolated established judicial reasoning to cover a variety of circumstances never considered by the courts. The resulting guidelines (which have, of course, no legal force) are fairly restrictive and it is possible, though by no means certain, that the courts would take a much more liberal line. In practice, a good many established charities regularly ignore the guidelines and, though they sometimes get ticked off, no sanctions seem ever to have been applied and certainly no charity has ever found itself in court. The real victims of the guidelines are would-be charities refused registration on the grounds that their pursuit of valid charitable purposes is too political.

The Goodman Committee recommended[4] that new legislation should provide that 'greater political activity should be permitted to charities' subject to the following guidelines:[5]

> (a) that political activity should not be an object of the charity nor a principal activity such that its charitable

object is in effect displaced by the extent of its political activity.

(b) that political activity should be and be seen to be ancillary to the object of the charity.

(c) that political activity should not include direct or indirect financial or other support for or opposition to any political party or individual or group seeking elective office, or any organisation having a political object.

At first blink this looks like a liberalising measure which would overrule the restrictive view sometimes taken by Commissioners. Examined more closely, however, it could be argued that what the Goodman Committee proposed would permit *less* political activity to charities than judicial precedents allow. For in no decided case have the courts held that 'political activity should not be a principal activity such that its charitable object is in effect displaced by the extent of its political activity'; nor do the Charity Commissioners' guidelines go so far as to rule out the possibility that a valid charitable object might be *entirely* pursued by political activity; indeed the case of the Upper Teesdale Defence Fund[6] shows that the Commissioners are prepared, in appropriate circumstances, to register just such a trust.

The House of Commons Expenditure Committee, in 1975, also favoured greater political freedom than the Charity Commissioners' guidelines seem to recommend. Avoiding the Goodman Committee's 'own goal' they urged the government to enshrine in legislation that

> All political activities in pursuit of a charitable object shall, so long as they remain subordinate to the main purposes of the charity, not endanger its charitable status.[7]

None of this, however, goes beyond a liberal construction of the law as it currently stands. What of peace, racial harmony and human rights – should they remain excluded as valid charitable objectives? At one stage, the Goodman Committee seems to have favoured a change in the law:

> The promotion of freedom of speech, justice, clemency for prisoners of conscience or freedom to worship may be worthy candidates for charitable status. And it may be inappropriate to apply the point made by Lord Parker in *Bowman v Secular Society* to such cases. For no one can seriously suggest any doubt that a proposed change would

> in these cases be for the public benefit. ... If an
> organisation satisfied the Charity Commissioners ... or the
> courts that it was acting in a non-partisan way, not seeking
> political power for itself but only seeking to influence those
> in power in pursuit of an object which on a reasonable value
> judgement was clearly for the benefit of the community –
> and some aspects at least of human rights would seem to us
> to come within this category – we can see a strong argument
> for allowing charitable status.[8]

But having uttered these stirring words the report never returns to
the theme. Its 'Conclusions and Recommendations'[9] contain no
hint of the issue and one searches in vain through the 'Guidelines
in Relation to the Meaning of Charitable Purposes' (see Appendix
2) for any mention of peace, racial harmony or human rights.

In the USA, the problem was tackled over twenty years ago by
extending the meaning of 'charitable' for the purposes of tax
concessions, beyond its meaning in law. Treasury regulation
501(c)(3), issued in 1959, accepts the decided cases but adds four
extra categories:

> Charitable defined. – The term 'charitable' is used in
> section 501(c)(3) in its generally accepted legal sense. ...
> Such term includes: Relief of the poor and distressed or of
> the underprivileged; advancement of religion; advance-
> ment of education or science; erection or maintenance of
> public buildings, monuments, or works; lessening of the
> burdens of Government; and promotion of social welfare
> by organisations designed to accomplish any of the above
> purposes, *or (i) to lessen neighborhood tensions; (ii) to
> eliminate prejudice and discrimination; (iii) to defend human
> and civil rights secured by law; or (iv) to combat community
> deterioration and juvenile delinquency.*' (italics added)

The advancement of peace does not specifically figure in this list
but there is no call for its appearance because American courts
have long accepted peace as a valid charitable object.[10] The
language used in Regulation 501(c)(3) might need to be translated
for the British context but change of this kind could eliminate
much of the discontent caused by restrictions on political
activities by charities. And to legitimise the promotion of peace,
racial harmony and human rights would require only a very short
Parliamentary Bill.

Although American law does not exclude peace, racial harmony
or human rights from charitable tax concessions, in certain other

respects it is considerably more restrictive than its English cousin. Full tax concessions are only granted to an organisation that does not 'devote more than an insubstantial part of its activities to attempts to influence legislation'.[11] However, the US *Tax Reform Act 1976* mitigated this by creating several tiers of voluntary organisations enjoying varying degrees of tax exemption. The top-tier bodies must not devote more than an insubstantial part of their expenditure to political activity and may, if they wish, opt for a set 'substantiality' criterion which allows them to devote up to 20 per cent of their expenditure to political activity. Second-tier bodies – known as 'action organisations' – have much greater political freedom but fewer tax privileges.

Obviously British charities would not welcome any 'substantiality' criterion being applied to eligibility for tax concessions but prefer to retain their existing rights to engage in substantial lobbying. But the concept of a second tier of organisations entitled to some but not all of the tax concessions enjoyed by charities might have some attraction for those bodies which currently get no concessions at all. Without going so far as the radical reforms proposed by the Charity Law Reform Committee such a change could mitigate the worst consequences of being excluded from charitable status.

Another step which would go some way to easing the lot of non-charitable, 'action organisations' would be to legislate for the automatic validation of 'purpose trusts'. Space does not permit a full discussion of this issue but although the courts have taken a more liberal line in recent years some trusts of 'imperfect obligation' are still disallowed; this does not benefit anybody very much and cramps the work of 'action organisations' which cannot obtain charitable status.

All the options discussed so far would require legislation. But a certain amount could be achieved even if legislation proved impossible to obtain. At minimum a great deal more could be done to help existing and would-be charities to understand better the existing law on political activity and what they may and may not do. Many organisations' difficulties could be avoided altogether if they were better informed about the law and its administration. Particularly useful here, to judge by recent soundings, would be effective advice and training on the setting up and management of dual-structure organisations – those which comprise linked charitable and non-charitable bodies.

Besides education, a wider debate among charities themselves and a renewed dialogue with the Charity Commissioners, judges and others who shape the evolution of the law, could help to establish a new climate of opinion in which any further whittling away of charities' scope for political activity would become unlikely and a liberal construction of the existing law advanced.

The various options outlined in the last few pages range from the radical to the regressive. This continuum of possible change may be summarised as follows:

1. *A completely new start* as proposed by the Charity Law Reform Committee; all NPDOs (non-profit-distributing organisations) receive the tax concessions currently available to charities.
2. *Only non-party political NPDOs* get tax concessions.
3. *Legislation for peace, racial harmony and human rights* as valid charitable objects.
4. *A new category of 'action organisations'*, entitled to limited tax concessions, introduced.
5. *The validation of all 'purpose trusts'* enacted by legislation.
6. *Charities allowed to engage in any political activity* provided it is a means to a non-political end.
7. *Debate and dialogue to create a more liberal interpretation of existing law* especially with respect to would-be charities seeking registration.
8. *Better advice and education* for existing and would-be charities.
9. *Retain status quo.*
10. *New restriction on charities' political activity.*

By no means everyone favours attempts to reform the law on 'charity and political activity'. Even among the more radical charities consulted in the preparation of this study there was considerable apprehension, well summed up in the comment: 'Don't rock the boat. The existing law is not ideal but it gives us quite a lot of freedom. If it was clarified we might end up with new restrictions.' To others this will seem a counsel of despair. Like Milton, in his famous speech to Parliament defending freedom of expression, they will plead, 'Give me the liberty to know, to utter, and to argue freely according to conscience, above all liberties'.

There is great variety of opinion. So before any further steps can be taken, charities and voluntary organisations need to debate among themselves just how far they feel it right to go. Little will change without at least a degree of consensus about what changes are needed. But if such consensus were found, it may be that legislation (if that were called for) would not be a hopeless cause. Free speech has many allies, not least in Parliament. For as Milton pointed out:

> What would ye do then? Should ye suppress all this flowering crop of knowledge and new light sprung up and yet springing daily in this city? – Believe it, Lords and Commons, they who counsel ye to such a suppressing do as good as bid ye suppress yourselves.[12]

A gloomier view would hold that the Charity Commissioners will not feel able to shift their ground at all, that pressures to clamp down on charities' freedom of speech will grow, and that before long a court case will restrict still further the existing scope for political activity. But that will not inhibit the bolder spirits who will take the point of Mrs Thatcher's comment on Tony Benn's description of the Falklands campaign as a 'tragic and unnecessary war':

> The right hon. Gentleman called it an unnecessary war. Tragic it may have been, but may I point out to him that he would not enjoy the freedom of speech that he put to such excellent use unless people had been prepared to fight for it.[14]

For as Barry Cox has abundantly documented

> Overall, civil liberty has, despite many individual setbacks, continued to grow in Britain, because as a people we have continuously exercised our civil rights. It is this continuous exercise, rather than legislation, which ultimately determines the quality of liberty. . . . We get the freedoms we deserve.[13]

And if charities' persistent straying from the guidelines ends with a court decision that involves a narrow construction of the existing law, then as Ulysses Grant is reported to have said in his inaugural speech as US President:

> I know no method to secure the repeal of bad or obnoxious laws so effective as their stringent execution.

THE REGULATION OF CHARITIES

Chapter 8 examined various aspects of the regulatory roles of the Charity Commissioners and the Inland Revenue. And it was clear that there is scope for some improvement in the way these 'gate-keepers' go about their business, in the control of abuses and in the general accountability of charities. The key issues identified included the role and character of the Charity Commission and the adequacy of its staffing complement; the obstacles to the modernisation of outmoded trusts and charitable purposes; the problematic character of registration along with the difficulties caused by the absence of registration in Scotland and Northern Ireland; the obstacles to any appeal from decisions by the 'gate-keepers'; the very patchy provision for the public accountability of charities; and the difficulties trusts and foundations encounter when they wish to make grants to non-charitable bodies.

Over the years there has been a plethora of suggestions for remedying such problems and to assess them all would be a formidable task. What follows ignores a fair number of proposals that seem to have overlooked completely such important considerations as the role of the Inland Revenue in regularly reviewing charities' accounts. But a full assessment, even of the more plausible proposals, would deserve a volume to itself. The most that can be done within the compass of the present enquiry is to sketch some of the principal arguments for or against the leading proposals for change.

The key to understanding why the role and character of the Charity Commission continues to arouse a certain amount of disquiet within the voluntary sector is that, for over a century, its remit was confined to endowed charities. Only since 1960 has it had any responsibility for the 'collecting charities' – voluntary organisations which derive their income from grants, sub-scriptions and donations rather than from a permanent endowment of capital. Apart from registration, much of the Commission's work is still concerned with charitable endow-ments and the result seems to be that the concerns and traditions of the Commission's staff tend to be somewhat different from those of the 'collecting charities'. Hence the persistent difficulties and misunderstandings.

Linked to all this is the question of the Commission's *staffing levels*. Many charities complain that dealings with the Commission are often subject to considerable delays and the only charitable explanation for this is that the Commission is understaffed. This would not be surprising given that while the voluntary sector has steadily grown over the last decade, the Commission has suffered staffing cuts of over 8 per cent.

Senior figures in the voluntary sector condemn this as a false economy; and certainly, given that the Commission is bound to maintain its statutory services, staffing restrictions stand in the way of any real development in its services to 'collecting charities'. The present government proclaims its commitment to 'voluntarism' but the current staffing level of the Commission is a real (if minor) impediment to the growth and development of the voluntary sector. So one option that needs to be considered is a change in the way the Commission is staffed.

With over a century's experience of dealing with the regulation of endowed charities, the Commission has refined and perfected its skills to the point where there seem to be few, if any, complaints. The one area that still seems to cause problems concerns the *modernisation of outmoded trusts and charitable purposes*. Despite initial optimism, the *Charities Act 1960* does not seem to have provided a wholly satisfactory method of ensuring the effective deployment of a host of small, ancient endowments. The best thought-out proposals for change are those enshrined in the *Neighbourhood Trusts Bill* recently introduced in Parliament; this failed for lack of time but the government may wish to consider ways of assisting its progress. More generally there is the question of the *cy-près* doctrine. The Nathan Committee recommended that the Commissioners, while not ignoring the original purpose of an endowment, should have powers to change its objects radically where circumstances made this appropriate. This recommendation was not adopted in the 1960 Act and that decision continues to block what common sense would sometimes seem to recommend. The *Neighbourhood Trusts Bill* would overcome the problem in connection with the amalgamation of small, local endowments but would not permit 'cy-not-so-près' schemes in other cases. Hence the legislative adoption of the Nathan Committee's proposed relaxation of the *cy-près* doctrine is a second serious candidate as an option for improving the scope for modernising outmoded trusts.

Earlier sections of this chapter have touched on various aspects of the *registration of charities* and noted the recent trend to a more liberal interpretation of case law by the Charity Commissioners; further moves in that direction would undoubtedly be warmly welcomed by many in the voluntary sector. So, too, would changes in staffing policies that would overcome the delays often encountered. Two further issues need consideration, however. First, there is the question of exemptions from registration. The exemption of charities which have no appreciable investment income (but which may have a large income from other sources) offers a sizeable loophole for abuse which arguably should be closed. Some would go further still and reject all exemptions whatsoever. It is true that the case for exempting certain élite bodies, such as Eton or the Oxbridge colleges, from the provisions of the 1960 Act may seem less obvious today than in 1960. But there is a strong case for exempting small local voluntary groups which do not have a sizeable income; and after twenty-two years of inflation, an income of £15 no longer seems a sensible ceiling for such exemption; it might be wise, moreover, not to introduce any new fixed ceiling but allow the Commission to readjust it from time to time.

The second issue is the absence of any register in Scotland and in Northern Ireland. The problems this can cause were discussed in chapter 8; here it must suffice simply to note that the voluntary sector in these two countries would, by and large, welcome the introduction of a registration system so that this must be a serious option for legislative reform.

One area where there seems to be almost universal agreement that change is desirable, is the somewhat hollow *right of appeal* against decisions by the Charity Commission or, for that matter, the Inland Revenue. In theory, any decision can be challenged in the courts; in practice, very few voluntary organisations would find it easy even to meet, let alone justify, the considerable expense of a court action. Not only is this rough justice, it is not necessarily good for the health of the law. The theory is that the law evolves by the court's decisions in particular cases; but if few cases come before the courts the motor of evolution is idle.

One solution which has commanded considerable support in the past[15] is the establishment of a 'Charities Tribunal' to hear such appeals. The Charity Commissioners have opposed the idea, however, on the grounds that it would merely add another loop through which organisations would have to pass for the resolution of points of law. Certainly it must be doubtful whether a tribunal would be cheap: complex legal issues cannot simply be ridden over rough-shod and the chances are that considerable expense would be necessary even if it did not fall to the appellant.

That being so, it might make more sense to use any resources that could be made available to fund appeals to the High Court and beyond. There has been and remains widespread support for 'legal aid' for such appeals[16] but the idea does not seem to have been very vigorously pursued. The 1979 Report of the Royal Commission on Legal Services recorded that

> We have had no evidence to suggest that legal aid should be available for corporate bodies, whether trading or non-trading.[17]

and by and large the report did not favour legal aid except for individuals.[18] It did, however, recommend the establishment of a 'suitor's fund' to reimburse costs incurred to determine an unsettled point of law of public importance:

> We think it appropriate that the resolution of points of law of public importance, which benefits the community as a whole, should be financed out of the public purse. In 1953 the Evershed Committee on Supreme Court Practice and Procedure (Cmnd. 8878) recommended that public funds should be made available for litigating points of law of exceptional public interest either at first instance or on appeal. We support this.[19]

A small beginning could be made by putting at the disposal of the Charity Commissioners a new pilot fund for subsidising key test cases; the implications for public expenditure need not be great. And if the government rejected this approach it might be right to reconsider the long-standing policy that no charges are made for Charity Commission services. Even a small charge – say £10 for each registration, order or scheme – would fund several appeals a year. Another possibility is that the Inland Revenue might expand its occasional practice of paying its opponents' costs in test cases. Again private funds might be made available as in the housing test case already mentioned.

One further option deserves a mention. It has long been the practice of the Charity Commissioners, sitting as a Board, to act in effect as an appellate tribunal, hearing 'appeals' against decisions by their own staff. (The Inland Revenue has analogous arrangements.) It has to be said, however, that the existence of this arrangement is not widely advertised and a strong case could be made that it should be much more widely known; the Commissioners' staff, for example, could, as a matter of routine, inform every organisation advised that it cannot be registered that its case may be heard by the Board. In addition, there might be a case for opening up the Board's hearings, giving 'appellants' a right to attend and have the case against them explained and justified. This might do a great deal to reduce the somewhat 'remote' image the Commission seems to have acquired in some quarters. It must also be said that this arrangement cannot substitute for an effective right of appeal beyond the Commission; one need not doubt the integrity of the Commissioners to question whether it fully meets the fundamental requirements of natural justice.

Turning to the issue of *accountability*, there have been many proposals that the Charity Commissioners should play a more active role in regularly scrutinising charities' financial accounts and that no charities should be exempted from filing regular returns. For the reasons given in chapter 8, however, most of these seem unlikely to achieve a great deal. On the contrary, there seems a good case for remedial legislation to remove the requirement that a rather arbitrary category of charities must annually submit accounts. That is not, of course, to say that the Commissioners should lose their power to *require* charities to provide annual accounts and other financial documents or their general powers of enquiry which should, if anything, be strengthened and developed. There would be no harm, for example, in a team of roving auditors which conducted spot checks on a random selection of charities *pour encourager les autres*.

A much wider and perhaps more interesting possibility would be to seek ways of increasing the *public* accountability of charities. For charities are not private bodies and there is no obvious reason why they should not simply be of benefit to the public but also *be seen* to confer a benefit. Members of the public do, of course, have access to accounts held by the Charity Commissioners, which establishes the principle, but these are much less complete than those held by the Inland Revenue. And as J. D. Livingston-Booth (late Director of the Charities Aid Foundation) has pointed out:

This raises the question of the public accountability of the Revenue in the case of public trusts. It hardly seems logical to follow a principle that a public body is only entitled to a tax privileged status because of its public nature and the application of its funds to wholly public purposes, and then to prohibit the Revenue from disclosing the very statements which provide public accountability of the use of the funds which would otherwise have been public revenue. In the United States of America all charities recognised by Internal Revenue are recorded and published in an Internal Revenue Listing and all accounts of public charities submitted to the Revenue are available to the public. There seems to be no valid reason for doing otherwise in this country.[20]

Livingston-Booth went on to assert that:

A basic principle that if charities are to receive a tax privileged status from the community they must be fully accountable to the community, is not yet generally accepted by all charities. I suggest that all charities with an annual income in excess of £100 should be required by law to have their accounts audited and to make them available to anyone seeking information on the application of their funds. This should be a continuing requirement of charitable status.[21]

Both these proposals would seem likely to do a great deal more to increase the *public* accountability of charities than vast piles of accounts gathering dust in the archives of the Charity Commission.

Finally, but almost more important than all the foregoing, there is the question of the difficulties faced by grant-making trusts and foundations which wish to give *funds to non-charitable bodies for charitable activities*. This is perfectly allowable in law but in practice the Inland Revenue often seems to require very detailed justification of such grants. That is not unreasonable, for the scope for abuse would otherwise be considerable, but the effect is to discourage what are frequently potentially valuable applications of charitable resources.

One way in which this problem can be tackled is for grants to be made through a second charitable body but that often merely shifts the burden of proof. There is a strong case for a body which specialises in this role to develop standard techniques and a continuing working relationship with the Inland Revenue. This could be taken on by the Charities Aid Foundation (CAF at present only makes grants to registered charities) which would need to establish a specialist department for this work. Alternatively, if that proved difficult, it might be necessary to create a new body to undertake this function. Or, in principle, the Charity Commissioners could take up a role of checking the credentials of non-charitable bodies undertaking charitable tasks; this would not be *ultra vires* since their general function is described in the 1960 Act as

> Promoting the effective use of charitable resources by encouraging the development of better methods of administration, *by giving charity trustees information or advice on any matter affecting the charity* and by investigating and checking abuses.[22]

A WAY FORWARD

A great many different issues and problems have been touched on in the last few pages; and it is difficult to believe that many people will feel that none of them need tackling. But which deserve priority, and how they should be tackled – these are questions on which it would be unrealistic to expect universal agreement and which need to be widely debated.

This study is intended to inform that debate, not pre-empt it. Hence no attempt has been made to advocate the priority of any particular issue or to recommend any particular option for change. But the study *is* intended as a first step in a long-term strategy aimed at preserving what is best in charity law and its administration and remedying what is less satisfactory. Such a strategy might begin by formulating an agenda for reform – a provisional shopping-list of problem areas and possible solutions. The next step could be twofold: debate and discussion within the voluntary sector, on the basis of that agenda with a view to reaching the widest possible consensus on what changes would be useful; and dialogue with the Charity Commissioners and others responsible for the law and its administration to establish what might be achieved without seeking legislation or decisions by the courts. Where necessary such a strategy would lead on to test cases in the courts or the promotion of suitable legislation or both.

That could be a long haul. And there will be those to whom debate, discussion and negotiations will seem unduly tame and unlikely to bear fruit. It may be, too, that to pursue such a strategy would be to court the fate of all who tilt at windmills. Perhaps, on the other hand, one should have some faith in the potential of dialogue and the capacity of our native legal genius (assisted by the legislature) to evolve equitable law.

AN ILLUSTRATIVE AGENDA

It would be difficult to spend an extended period examining issues such as these without forming some opinions on what might be the most appropriate changes. But those cannot be more than one person's value judgements, tempered by an assessment both of what a broader range of opinion favours and of what seems likely to be possible as opposed to merely desirable. That said, an illustrative agenda for reform may help to focus discussion even if it must be stressed that what follows is no more than a very tentative first stab. The ten issues chosen are those which have come up most often in the course of interviews and discussions with a wide range of existing and would-be charities and other interested parties. The first five could, at least in principle, be tackled by administrative changes, by education or by both; and there can be no doubt that a great deal could be achieved by these means. The remainder would probably require legislation though some might be dealt with by a test case in the courts.

ADMINISTRATIVE CHANGE AND EDUCATION

1. Meeting new needs or old needs in new ways. Social and economic changes throw up new attitudes and problems which do not fit readily into the charity law tradition. Areas where problems seem to occur include unemployment, advice-giving, housing, sport, amateur art, ethical and moral societies, children in care, overseas aid (other than poverty, education and religion), fringe medicine, 'intermediary' agencies, community work, environmental issues, trading, self-help groups and participative management styles (co-operatives). A more open attitude by the Charity Commission (and the courts) could help a great deal. So could a voluntary world better informed about how to operate within existing case law.

2. Campaigning and lobbying. Many voluntary organisations are woefully ill informed about the law on charities and political activity – there is a real need for education in this area. But the law itself is far from clear and the Charity Commissioners' interpretation of it not unchallengeable. Discussion and dialogue could help to create a more liberal climate within the existing legal precedents where any form of campaigning was permissible provided it was in furtherance of 'non-political' purposes.

3. Registration. Ways could be found of making this much quicker and less adversarial. And applicants would also be helped by a better system of advocacy and advice: the voluntary sector needs to develop this.

4. A right of appeal. It could usefully be more widely known that applicants and others dealing with the Charity Commissioners' staff may appeal to the Commissioners sitting as a board; moreover that 'tribunal' could operate more openly. A 'legal aid' pilot fund for appeals to the High Court would be a major advance.

5. Charitable work by non-charities. Trusts and foundations often find it difficult to give grants to non-charities for charitable purposes. New arrangement could be developed to deal with this not infrequent problem, either based on existing bodies or by creating new ones.

CHANGES IN THE LAW

6. Excluded but publicly beneficial purposes. Over the years certain aims and objectives have been held by the courts not to count as charitable purposes. These include the promotion of peace, racial harmony and human rights as well as various aspects of the areas listed at paragraph 1 such as advice-giving and the general welfare of children in care. The lack of any decided cases impedes developments in certain areas such as environmental issues and overseas aid. Test cases, or amending legislation (on the lines of the *Recreational Charities Act 1958*) could be introduced to bring all or some of these within the law.

7. Regulation of charities. The *Charities Act 1960* was originally intended to regulate *endowed* charities but extends to those without endowments; the results are sometimes anomalous or even counter-productive. Remedial measures might include (i) removing the registration exemption from charities without investment income while substantially raising the threshold for exemption from the current £15 ceiling; (ii) abandoning the requirement for regular return of accounts to the Charity Commissioners but providing public access to any annual accounts held by the Commissioners or the Inland Revenue; (iii) requiring all charities except the smallest to prepare audited accounts and to make them available to all members of the public on request.

8. Registration in Scotland and Northern Ireland. The establishment of central registers with similar requirements to this country (bearing in mind what is said in the preceding paragraph).

9. Modernisation of charities. A good many ancient endowments might be more usefully applied if (i) the Neighbourhood Trusts Bill recently introduced in Parliament were passed; (ii) the *cy-près* doctrine was relaxed as sugested by the Nathan report but not implemented in the *Charities Act 1960*.

10. Public benefit. A more logical conception of public benefit would (i) withhold tax concessions from most charities which benefit entirely or primarily the well-to-do; (ii) not allow the establishment of new charitable trusts for poor relations.

These are *not* recommendations. Some will wish to add to the list, some to delete; a few will reject it out of hand. But that is its purpose: an agenda for discussion.

Conclusion:
The Spirit of Charity

Want is only one of five giants on the road of reconstruction and in some ways the easiest to attack. The others are Disease, Ignorance, Squalor and Idleness.

(Sir William Beveridge)[1]

'What giants?' asked Sancho Panza. 'Those you see there', replied his master, 'with their long arms. Some giants have them about six miles long.' 'Take care, your worship', said Sancho; 'those things over there are not giants but windmills'. . . . 'It is quite clear', replied Don Quixote, 'that you are not experienced in this matter of adventures'. . . . Then, covering himself with his shield and putting his lance in the rest, he urged Rocinante forward at a full gallop and attacked the nearest windmill, thrusting his lance into the sail. But the wind turned it with such violence that it shivered his weapon in pieces, dragging the horse and his rider with it, and sent the knight rolling badly injured across the plain. . . .

'Happy the age and happy the times on which the ancients bestowed the name of golden . . . because the people of those days did not know those two words thine *and* mine. *In that blessed age all things were held in common. . . . All was peace then, all amity, all concord. . . . Justice pursued her own proper purposes, undisturbed and unassailed by favour and interest which so impair, restrain and pervert her today. The law did not then depend on the judge's nice interpretations, for there were none to judge or to be judged.*

'But now in this detestable age of ours . . . as time rolled on and wickedness increased, the order of knights errant was founded . . . to defend maidens, relieve widows and succour orphans and the needy.'

(Cervantes)[2]

Don Quixote's speech after his disastrous encounter with the 'giants' reminds us that his escapades, however wrong-headed, were always part of a quest for social justice, motivated by a spirit of charity. Charity in this broad sense – 'love thy neighbour as thyself' – remains a powerful if often unconscious influence even in these secular times. For whatever doctrines, myths and ritual practices may be rejected, there abides a certain fascination and respect for the principle of 'equal and unconditional concern for the welfare of every fellow human being'.

Charity – neighbour-love – is not simply a matter of feeling and emotion; it is a principle that engages the intellect and requires a deliberate effort of will. To love one's enemies or to cherish the unattractive must often cut across any natural emotion. But although not sentimental, the spirit of charity is fundamentally romantic inasmuch as its purpose is derived not from things as they actually are but more from one's imagination of what they should be, ideally.

And because charity has *equal* concern for every fellow human being it requires equity – a justice that transcends the strict letter of the law and upholds what is reasonable and fair rather than what is merely legal. Alms-giving has its place but charity cannot rest content simply to drop pennies in collecting tins, ignoring social injustice and oppression. The problem is vividly summed up in Tolstoy's caustic verdict on those who maintain that charity can be divorced from social justice:

> I sit on a man's back, choking him and making him carry me, and yet assure myself and others that I am very sorry for him and wish to ease his lot by all possible means – except by getting off his back.[3]

Hence charity, when it implies social justice, will often tend to threaten vested interests; and they, in turn, will seek out ways of taming such inconvenient aspirations. Various examples were touched on in chapter 7 and none, perhaps, more striking than the recent history of charity and overseas aid.

Money pours in for famine appeals and nobody would wish it otherwise. But those actually tackling the problems in the third world know from bitter experience that this is only a small part of what is needed. Famine relief is only one possible response to 'world hunger' and most overseas aid charities would argue that the problems can only deteriorate unless it is complemented by other approaches. Figure 1 (p. 173) sets out four different responses to 'world hunger'. The second approach is winning wider acceptance as more and more people realise that teaching the hungry to fish is a more lasting solution than simply giving them fish. Less widespread, however, is the realisation that even fishing lessons will not be much use if the river is polluted and there is no access to markets where fish can be sold to pay for other necessities. Yet charity cannot ignore the fact that injustice, oppression and exploitation underlie more hunger than lack of technical skills or natural calamities. And it is striking how, as the churches, in particular, confront the problems of the third world and reach back to their roots to rediscover the close connection between charity and social justice, they encounter a mixture of disbelief and angry opposition.

Having said all that, concern for social justice is not the pinnacle of charity as the fourth column of Figure 1 makes clear. The spirit of charity has a wider and more joyful outlook: it looks beyond the struggle for human rights and social justice, essential as that is, to a world in which human nature itself has been transformed, peace, amity and concord prevail, and all willingly share the fruits of their labour: a voluntary social justice. An impossible dream, perhaps, but the vision at the heart of charity, nevertheless. For while Moses held that social justice was the price of freedom, his successors gradually came to the view that social justice can never be fully realised without a radical and widespread change of heart.

But while it may be true that even the best of laws and the widest of civil liberties cannot achieve a fully just and free society, bad laws and the suppression of civil rights are obstacles to charity's wider aspirations. And time and again the small, still voice of conscience has compelled protest, however dangerous, however inconvenient to those in positions of power and authority. For the spirit of charity cannot be muzzled – it will always spontaneously cry out against injustice and oppression.

Twentieth-century judges, both in this country and abroad, have gradually whittled away the freedom of speech of organised, 'legal' charity; and there is a real danger that still more could be lost unless the substantial freedom that remains is more vigorously defended than it has been up to now. And that defence may come too late. But even if organised charities' freedom of speech was severely curtailed or abolished altogether, all would not be lost. It is unthinkable that, in Britain, freedom of speech could be taken away from non-charitable voluntary organisations; and if tax concessions became the dummy firmly clamped into charities' mouths, silencing all protest, some at least would prefer to render unto the State such taxes as the State dictated.

For whatever judges may rule that 'charity' means within the letter of the law, the spirit of charity (shorn, if need be of tax concessions) will retain its concern for social justice and the

Figure 1 – DIFFERENT RESPONSES TO 'WORLD HUNGER'

Four Types of Response

	1	2	3	4
Problem	Famine	Underdevelopment	Exploitation	Alienation of poor *and* rich
Need	More food now	More development	More social justice	Genuine community
Visual Image	Starving child	Parched earth	Wealthy landowner; Western extravagant consumption	Bloated arms budget
Remedy	Relief aid	Assistance for self-help	Fundamental changes in socio-economic order	Repentance; a change of heart at all levels
Life-style Response	Give surplus money, food	Give money, technical aid, seek to understand	Support human rights movements abroad; political education and pressure at home	Co-operative living; austerity, voluntary poverty
Long-term	Dependence	Self-reliance	Shift of power and wealth	Rich find *their* humanity as well as poor

Different Meanings of 'Development Education'

	1	2	3	4
Subject	Need for relief overseas	Development projects overseas	Injustice, oppression exploitation both overseas and at home	Need for total liberation of all
Method	I tell or show you (because you do not know)		You and I together search for knowledge (dialogue)	

(*Adapted from a chart by Brian Wren, after Charles Lutz*)

173

improvement of the human condition. Its track record in promoting progress is unrivalled – the abolition of slavery, humane penology, decent working hours and conditions, and virtually all our modern welfare services. But those hard-won advances leave giant evils still to be tackled. Millions of children and women and men around this planet still live in conditions of appalling poverty, brutality and degradation. And while that hell on earth dwarfs the inadequacies of our own Welfare State, we still remain a very long way from meeting the needs of the third world in our own backyard.

Charity – romantic but unsentimental concern for the fate of every fellow human being, equal and unconditional love of every neighbour – cannot sit back quietly in the face of so much misery, suffering and violence. The spirit of charity rebels, for as that great rebel William Blake once wrote,[5]

> Love seeketh not itself to please,
> Nor for itself hath any care,
> But for another gives its ease
> And builds a Heaven in Hell's despair.

APPENDIX 1

Charities and the law in Scotland and Northern Ireland

The law in Scotland differs in many ways from the law of England and Wales; and the terms 'charity' and 'charitable' do not have exactly the same meaning in Scots law as they do south of the border. The law in Northern Ireland is much closer to the English system but is nevertheless governed by Irish rather than English legislation.

Scotland has no agency corresponding to the English Charity Commission and no general system for the registration of charities, although educational endowments must be registered with the Scottish Education Department which also has powers to modernise out-of-date trusts. Non-educational charities must apply to the Court of Session for *cy-près* schemes and will usually have to pay several hundred pounds to achieve modernisation.

There is no central register in Northern Ireland, either, but the Department of Finance exercises most of the other powers allocated in England to the Charity Commissioners.

These differences are not, however, quite as significant as they seem at first because, so far as taxation and rating relief is concerned – and these are after all the chief attraction of charitable status – the English definition of charity applies throughout the United Kingdom. There are some local differences – in Northern Ireland, for example, charities are entitled to 100 per cent rates relief, not 50 per cent as in England and Wales. But the *principles* of fiscal relief are exactly the same and the same conditions have to be met.

There is fairly strong support, both in Scotland and Northern Ireland, for the establishment of some form of registration of charities. This issue is discussed in chapter 8 where it is concluded, however, that the advantages of a central register may not be as great as is sometimes thought.

APPENDIX 2

The Goodman Committee Guidelines in Relation to the Meaning of Charitable Purposes

The following guidelines are intended to be in substitution for the guidelines contained in the preamble to the Statute of Charitable Uses 1601 and the classification of charities contained in the speech of Lord Macnaghten in Pemsel's case. They do not obviate the need for compliance with other criteria of charity such as benefit to a sufficient section of the community and exclusion generally of private profit. The categories of charity contained in the guidelines are not intended to be either exhaustive or immutable but only to be a statement of the types of activity which at the present time should come properly and eminently within the scope of charitable purposes. Any of the said purposes shall be in principle charitable if carried out by UK charities operating abroad.

The expression 'charitable purposes' shall include and shall be deemed always to have included the following purposes, that is to say:-

(a) The relief of poverty howsoever caused and its prevention in suitable cases.

(b) The relief and prevention of sickness and disability, both physical and mental, including:-

   (i) The provision and staffing of hospitals, nursing and convalescent homes and clinics;

   (ii) The promotion of medical research;

   (iii) The provision of advice, treatment or comfort;

   (iv) The establishment of homes, workshops or other centres for the disabled or the mentally or physically handicapped or any other disadvantaged or needy persons.

(c) The relief of the suffering and distress or disability caused by old age, including the provision of homes for the care and maintenance of the old and of housing for old people adapted to their special needs.

(d) The relief of distress caused by natural disasters or sudden catastrophes.

(e) The advancement of education, including:-

  (i) The provision of schools, colleges, universities, and other like institutions;

 (ii) The establishment of professorships, fellowships, and lectureships;

(iii) The provision of scholarships, bursaries and prizes;

(iv) The provision of physical training and sports for young persons both within and without such institutions;

 (v) The education of the public generally (including those not engaged in full-time study at school, colleges, universities, and other like institutions); provided that no attempt is made to influence the public by propaganda.

(f) The promotion of research in any field of knowledge seriously deserving to be researched into, whereby the common stock of knowledge can be increased provided that the fruits of such research are intended to be (and are) made available to the public.

(g) The advancement of science (here meaning all recognised branches of learning, and not merely the natural sciences), and the maintenance of institutions therefor, including the support and maintenance of learned societies.

(h) The nurturing of public taste in aesthetic matters, including art, music, literature and fine craftsmanship including facilities for their practice.

(i) The provision and maintenance of museums and art galleries.

(j) The advancement of religion (here meaning belief in and reverence for a divine power) and the practice of the worship of that divinity, including:

  (i) The organisation and carrying out of religious instruction, pastoral and missionary work at home and overseas;

 (ii) The provision and maintenance of buildings for such worship or any other religious use;

(iii) The payment of stipends to and the provision of houses for ministers of religion, their widows and dependent children; and

(iv) Other purposes tending to promote the moral or spiritual welfare of the community.

(k) The advancement of ethical and moral teachings and studies.

(l) The provision of social welfare services for those in need of them.

(m) The provision of housing for those in special need.

(n) The protection (including preservation and improvement) of the national heritage whether physical, environmental, artistic, cultural or otherwise.

(o) The promotion of sport and recreation, including the provision of facilities for recreation within the meaning of the Recreational Charities Act 1958.

(p) The welfare of children including prevention of cruelty to them.

(q) The promotion of the social welfare of the family.

(r) The welfare of animals including prevention of cruelty to them.

(s) Rehabilitation and resettlement.

(t) The establishment in life of young people.

(u) The establishment of organisations to assist sections of the community with special needs, for example, one-parent families, single persons with dependants, battered spouses, specially gifted children and immigrants.

(v) Advice giving in suitable circumstances.

(w) The provision of public works for the benefit of the community and the protection of the lives and property of the community (to the extent that these services are inadequately provided for by the State).

(x) The advancement and improvement of the standards of efficiency of industry, commerce and agriculture.

(y) The maintenance and improvement of the efficiency of the fighting forces and the police force and their welfare.

(z) Gifts for the benefit of the inhabitants of a particular place or for the benefit of a particular section of the community.

Charity Commission Guidelines on Political Activities

A. EXTRACT FROM THE ANNUAL REPORT FOR 1969

Political Activities by Charities

7. We have remarked from time to time in our previous reports on the difficulties which face us, particularly in the discharge of our quasi-judicial functions, in applying the law of charity to new activities which grow out of the constantly changing needs of society. In a world in which the pace of social change seems ever to be increasing we shall inevitably continue to be faced with new or extended activities, the charitable nature of which has never been the subject of consideration by the courts. We are, however, often bound to consider how far such activities may properly be regarded as consonant with charitable purposes both in connexion with our responsibility for registering charities and with our function of giving advice to charity trustees.

8. One contemporary development which has given us some concern has been the increasing desire of voluntary organisations for "involvement" in the causes with which their work is connected. Many organisations now feel that it is not sufficient simply to alleviate distress arising from particular social conditions or even to go further and collect and disseminate information about the problems they encounter. They feel compelled also to draw attention as forcibly as possible to the needs which they think are not being met, to rouse the conscience of the public to demand action and to press for effective official provision to be made to meet those needs. As a result "pressure groups", "action groups" or "lobbies" come into being. But when a voluntary organisation which is a charity seeks to develop such activities it nearly always runs into difficulties through going beyond its declared purposes and powers. No charity should, of course, undertake any activity unless it is reasonably directed to achieving its purposes and is within the powers conferred by the

charity's governing instrument.

9. This development has resulted in our having to consider in a number of different contexts the extent to which individual charities may properly engage in activities which may be described generally as of a political nature, and further whether it is possible for us to indicate in a general way what in our view are the pitfalls for which charities must be on the lookout. We endeavour in the following paragraphs to give some guidance on this matter, but we would emphasise that the law is based on a limited number of decided cases and there is some danger in trying to stretch them to cover the whole of the ground. In the last resort any particular case must be judged on all the circumstances pertaining to it, and what we say below must be regarded as guidance of only the most general kind which may well need to be modified when applied to individual cases. We are always ready to give our opinion on any particular case where the trustees are in doubt, although many charities likely to come into contact with this problem will have their own legal advisers to whom they should turn for advice in the first instance.

10. It is a well-established principle of charity law that a trust for the attainment of a political object is not a valid charitable trust and that any purpose with the object of influencing the legislature is a political purpose. Thus no organisation can be a charity and at the same time include among its purposes the object of bringing influence to bear directly or indirectly on Parliament to change the general law of the land. If the governing instrument of an organisation were to give it power, other than in a way merely ancillary to some charitable purpose, to play a part in bringing political pressure to bear, that by itself would throw serious doubt on the organisation's claim to be a charity. Thus it is very unlikely that it will lie within any charity's purposes and powers to sponsor action groups or bring pressure to bear on the government to adopt or alter a particular line of action. In the past it was recognised that such activity lay well outside the true field of charity although, as will be mentioned below, there are other more traditional approaches to Parliament and to the government that have long been accepted as perfectly proper for a charity. Today, however, it seems that the limitations on action of this kind are not always recognised by those responsible for running charities.

11. Those trustees who feel that their charity should become

involved in the political field frequently seek to justify such action as coming within the field of "education". In our report for 1966 we mentioned the misuse of this word in the governing instruments of some organisations applying for registration as charities. Increasingly we are confronted by attempts to represent as educational a variety of activities which are primarily of a propagandist nature and which accordingly cannot be accepted as coming within the meaning of the "advancement of education" as it is used in charity law. There is a similar tendency for those registered charities which have as a subsidiary object the education of the public in the particular aspect of charity with which the organisation is concerned (for instance the need for the relief of poverty in under-developed countries) to overstep the boundary of what might properly be described as education and pass outside their declared purposes into the field of propaganda. There is obvious difficulty in determining exactly where this boundary lies but if a charity with general objects, such as the relief of poverty or distress, issues literature urging the government to take a particular course or organises sympathisers to apply pressure for that purpose to their elected representatives, we think it is clear that the boundary has been overstepped.

12. We would emphasise that it is not for us to judge whether the object of a propagandist or political activity is morally or socially right or wrong although we can appreciate the reasons why some charities feel a moral obligation to attempt to influence policies. We are concerned simply with the law of charity and with seeking to ensure that funds which are impressed with charitable trusts are used for the purposes of those trusts and not for other purposes which could not be recognised as charitable. However small the proportion of the income of a charity which may be used in this way, we believe that the charity will be led into difficulties if it appears to be giving its support to any objects that are not strictly within its charitable purposes.

13. We have, where it has seemed to us to be necessary, brought these considerations to the notice of individual charities. We are aware, however, that there may be other charities, which have perhaps not yet discussed their problems with us, and which are hesitating about promoting their objects by activities which might perhaps be considered to be political activities. We believe that it might help charities to realise what they have power to do if we point the contrast by giving some examples of such activities

which we believe can justifiably be regarded as being proper for a charity. These examples fall into three classes, the first and third of which present little difficulty. The first class comprises those examples in which it is the government itself which is investigating or has propounded proposals for changes in the law. Government officials frequently seek advice and information from those who are responsible for running charities and the charities quite properly respond. Similarly by publishing a green or white paper the government may impliedly invite comments from the public generally and a charity may justifiably avail itself of such an invitation to make any comments which may appear to be useful. Again when a parliamentary bill has been published a charity will be justified in supplying relevant information to a member of either House and such arguments to be used in debate as it believes will assist the furtherance of its purposes. So also there can be other cases, not involving legislation, in which a charity is entitled to persuade a Member to support its cause in Parliament, for instance, where the question arises whether a government grant is to be made or continued to a particular charity.

14. The second class of examples, which includes those in which the charity itself or with others wishes to put forward proposals for changes in the law, can be more difficult to justify. It is probably unobjectionable for a charity to present to a government department a reasoned memorandum advocating changes in the law provided that in doing so the charity is acting in furtherance of its purposes. On the other hand, a charity can only spend its funds on the promotion of public general legislation if in doing so it is exercising a power that is merely ancillary to its charitable purposes. But here again difficulty arises in defining the boundary between what is merely ancillary and what amounts to adopting a new purpose in itself. A charity would be well advised to seek advice either from its legal advisers or from us before undertaking any such activities.

15. Finally, the third class of examples comprise cases where, although Parliament is involved, it appears to us that the reason for approaching it is not to be regarded as political. This, for instance, includes legislation that is only intended to confer enabling powers, such as the Sharing of Church Buildings Act which is mentioned in paragraphs 36 to 39 of this report. By supporting the passage of this Act the various charities involved

were seeking to obtain wider powers to carry out their purposes. Similarly, virtually all private bills are free from taint of political activities. A private bill is in the nature of litigation as much as of legislation and the action of supporting or opposing such a bill resembles a court action and nearly always has no political tinge. We feel, therefore, that the principle laid down by the courts that a political object is not a charitable purpose should not be extended in such a way as to deny to a charity that right to promote or oppose private legislation which is enjoyed by public and private bodies in general. Thus in every session some charities, with our consent under section 19(7) of the Charities Act, promote private bills which may set out to alter the constitution of the charity or to give it powers which only Parliament can confer. An example of such a bill in the present session is the National Trust Bill. The case mentioned in paragraphs 23 and 24 of this report provides an example of a charity which in order to realise its charitable purposes played a part in opposing a private bill.

16. There are two general points which we should like to mention in concluding this section of our report. First, if the trustees of a charity do stray into the field of political activity their action will be in breach of trust and those responsible for the action could be called on at law to recoup to the charity any of its funds which have been spent outside its purposes. Moreover a charity is not entitled to tax relief on income which is not applied to charitable purposes. But the fact that political action had been taken in the name of the charity would not affect its status as a charity nor constitute a reason for removing it from the register of charities. If, however, doubt had been cast on the correctness of the original registration removal might be considered by us or by the High Court on an appeal by any other body interested. Secondly we think it should also be borne in mind that if charities step outside the sphere of activities to which the law confines them they may not only prejudice the support they receive from some people, who could resent the new activities, but they may also eventually endanger the privileged position which charities as a whole have been accorded by the state. The attempts now being made in the United States to curtail the privileges enjoyed by charitable foundations there result in part from allegations that some of those foundations have been using their funds for purposes which are essentially political.

B. EXTRACT FROM THE ANNUAL REPORT FOR 1981

Political Activities by Charities

50. During the year we continued to receive some complaints about alleged political activities by charities and it seems timely, therefore, in the light of the judgement in the Amnesty International Trust case, mentioned in paragraphs 38 to 49, to supplement the advice we gave in paragraphs 13 to 16 of our report for 1969.

51. As we have emphasised in previous reports, the extent to which it is permissible for charities to promote, support or take part in political activities is not an area in which it is possible to lay down hard and fast rules. Each case has to be considered individually in the light of all the relevant circumstances and trustees should not hesitate to consult their legal advisers or seek our advice. The law has to be derived from a small number of decided cases. It is possible to deduce certain basic principles, and it may be helpful initially to set these out (as they were, in our view, before the Amnesty case which has confirmed and amplified the position):-

 (i) A trust for the attainment of a political object is not charitable since the Court has no way of judging whether a proposed change in the law will or will not be for the public benefit – *Bowman v Secular Society Ltd.* [1917] A.C. 406; 442.

 (ii) To promote changes in the law, or maintenance of the existing law, is a political purpose and not charitable – *re Hopkinson* [1949] 1 All E.R. 346; 350.

 (iii) To seek, not necessarily particular legislation, but a particular line of political administration or policy, is a political purpose and is not charitable – *re Hopkinson* [1949] 1 All E.R. 346; 352.

 (iv) Political propaganda in the guise of education is not charitable – *re Hopkinson* [1949] 1 All E.R. 346.

 (v) The word "political" is not necessarily confined to party politics. Any purpose of influencing legislation is a political purpose and is not charitable – *Inland Revenue Commissioners v. Temperance Council of Christian Churches of England and Wales* [1926] 10 T.C. 748.

(vi) A trust for the education of the public in one particular set of political principles is not charitable (although education in political matters generally could be) – *Bonar Law Memorial Trust v. Inland Revenue Commissioners* [1933] 17 T.C. 508.

(vii) Although an association for promoting some change in the law cannot itself be a charity (see (i) and (ii) above), an association would not necessarily lose its right to be considered a charity if, as a matter of construction, the promotion of legislation were one among other lawful purposes ancillary to good charitable purposes: it is a question of degree – *National Anti-Vivisection Society v. Inland Revenue Commissioners* [1943-47] 28 T.C. 358; 368; 378 (HL).

(viii) Research, to be charitable, must be directed to increasing the store of communicable knowledge in a public, as opposed to a private, way – *re Hopkins' Will Trusts* [1965] Ch. 669.

52. In addition to removing any doubts on the question whether the constraints on domestic political activities extend to attempts to influence the politics and administrative policies of foreign countries, the Amnesty case has served to re-assert the validity of the principles set out above.

53. The implications for charity trustees of the present state of the law – as confirmed by the Amnesty case – may be summarised as:-

(i) Trustees who stray too far into the field of political activity:

(a) risk being a breach of trust;

(b) risk being held personally liable to repay to the charity the funds spent on such activity; and

(c) risk losing some tax relief for their charity, since this may be claimed only in respect of income applied to charitable purposes.

(ii) Political activity by the trustees would not necessarily affect the charitable status of the institution or be a reason for removing it from the Central Register of Charities; *but*

(iii) If the trustees could validly claim that the expressed purposes of the institution were wide enough to cover political activities, doubt would arise whether those purposes were exclusively charitable and, if the institution was registered as a charity, upon the correctness of the registration.

54. The following guidelines may be of help for the general guidance of charity trustees:-

(i) A charity should undertake only those activities which can reasonably be said to be directed to achieving its purposes and which are within the powers conferred by its governing instrument;

(ii) To avoid doubt being cast on the claim of an institution to be a charity, its governing instrument should not include power to exert political pressure except in a way that is merely ancillary to a charitable purpose. Whether a particular provision in the governing instrument of an institution is a substantive object or an ancillary object or power is a matter of the construction of the instrument. In general, what is ancillary is that which furthers the work of the institution, not something that will procure the performance of similar work by, for example, the Government of the day.

(iii) The powers and purposes of a charity should not include power to bring pressure to bear on the Government to adopt, alter, or maintain a particular line of action.It is permissible for a charity, in furtherance of its purposes, to help the Government to reach a decision on a particular issue by providing information and argument, but the emphasis must be on rational persuasion.

(iv) A charity can spend its funds on the promotion of public general legislation only if in doing so it is exercising a power which is ancillary to and in furtherance of its charitable purposes.

(v) If a charity's objects include the advancement of education, care should be taken not to overstep the boundary between education and propaganda in promoting that object: for example, the distribution of literature urging the Government to take a particular course, or urging sympathisers to apply pressure to Members of Parliament for that purpose, would not be education in the charitable sense.

(vi) A charity which includes the conduct of research as one of its objects must aim for objectivity and balance in the method of conducting research projects; and in publishing the results of the research must aim to inform and educate the public, rather than to influence political attitudes or inculcate a particular attitude of mind.

(vii) Charities, whether they operate in this country or overseas, must avoid:-

(a) Seeking to influence or remedy those causes of poverty which lie in the social, economic and political structures of countries and communities.

(b) Bringing pressure to bear on a government to procure a change in policies or administrative practices, (for example, on land reform, the recognition of local trade unions, human rights, etc.).

(c) Seeking to eliminate social, economic, political or other injustice.

55. Unless its governing instrument precludes it from doing so, a charity may, generally speaking, freely engage in activities of the following kinds:-

(i) Where the Government or a governmental agency is considering or proposing changes in the law and invites comments or suggestions from charities, they can quite properly respond.

(ii) Where a Green or White Paper is published by the Government, a charity may justifiably comment.

(iii) Where a Parliamentary Bill has been published, a charity is justified in supplying to Members of either House such relevant information and arguments to be used in debate as it believes will assist the furtherance of its purposes.

(iv) Where a Bill would give a charity wide powers to carry out its purposes, it can quite properly support the passage of the Bill; and it can support or oppose any Private Bill relevant to its purposes, since private legislation does not normally have a political character.

(v) Where a question arises as to whether a Government grant is to be made or continued to a particular charity, the charity is entitled to seek to persuade Members of Parliament to support its cause.

(vi) Where such action is in furtherance of its purposes, a charity may present to a Government Department a reasoned memorandum advocating changes in the law.

56. In suggesting these guidelines to trustees, we are not purporting to say that certain activities are morally, socially, or politically wrong or undesirable or that they ought not to be done; but that it is not permissible for them to be carried out by a charity, according to our understanding of the law. We are concerned only with the law and must seek to ensure that funds and other property impressed with charitable trusts are used for the purposes of those trusts and not for purposes which the law does not accept as charitable. We are always willing to give further advice on any specific problem a charity may have in this connection; for example, on the distinction between education and propaganda, or between an ancillary purpose and a main purpose, and to consider the drafts of any publications such as advertisements, appeals, newsletters, etc, on which trustees have doubts.

Notes

INTRODUCTION

1. *Report of The Charity Commissioners for England and Wales for the year 1969* (HMSO, 1970), p.5.

2. *Idem, 1981* (HMSO, 1982), p.21.

3. *Nathan Report: Report of the Committee on the Law and Practice relating to charitable Trusts.* Cmd. 8710 (HMSO, 1952).

4. *Charity Law – only a new start will do* (Charity Law Reform Committee, 1974). CLRC is now disbanded and the leaflet out of print.

5. *Tenth Report from the Expenditure Committee: Charity Commissioners and their Accountability* (HMSO, 1975), 2 volumes.

6. *Charity Law and Voluntary Organisations: Report of the Goodman Committee* (Bedford Square Press, 1976).

7. *Public Schools Commission: First Report* (HMSO, 1968), 2 volumes.

8. *The Times*, 27 May 1981, p.1; 25 June 1981, p.1.

9. Independent Schools Information Service. *Newsletter*, No.31, Spring 1982. A survey of 5000 SDP members for the television programme *Weekend World* found that 28 per cent would leave the schools as they are, 54 per cent would take away the tax advantages their charitable status confers, and 18 per cent would integrate them into the State system.

10. *Re Tetley, National Provincial and Union Bank of England v. Tetley* [1923], 1 C.H. at p.266.

11. N. Webb and R. Wybrew, *The Gallup Report* (Sphere, 1982), p.154. In a Gallup poll conducted in 1981 'only 13 per cent of the public saw Britain as a Christian society, and 76 per cent saw it as a multi-faith society. Moreover, 55 per cent saw this as a good thing, and only 23 per cent as bad in any way'.

12. *Ibid.*, p.151. Some 36 per cent believed in a personal God, 37 per cent in some kind of spirit or lifeforce, 15 per cent professed agnosticism and 12 per cent rejected the idea of any spirit, God or lifeforce.

13. *Ibid.*, p.153.

14. *Ibid.*, p.155.

15. *Bowman v. Secular Society* [1917], A.C. 406.

16. The most useful introduction is *Charitable Status: A Practical Handbook* by Andrew Philips and Keith Smith (Inter-Action Imprint, 1982). This provides a reliable and readable guide to setting up and registering a new charity; it also includes a useful booklist. At the other end of the spectrum, the standard work on charity law is *Tudor on Charities* by D.H. McMullen and others (Sweet and Maxwell, 1967) although a useful (and more up to date) alternative is H. Picarda, *The Law and Practice Relating To Charities* (Butterworth, 1977). Both of these are expensive reference books and non-lawyers would probably find D.G. Cracknell's much shorter (and far cheaper) textbook, *Law Relating to Charities* (Oyez, 1982) the best bet. None of the foregoing goes at all deeply into the policy issues surrounding charity law but Michael Chesterman's excellent *Charities, Trusts and Social Welfare* (Weidenfeld and Nicholson, 1979) provides a penetrating analysis and is highly recommended to those interested in pursuing further the issues treated here.

1. LET MY PEOPLE GO

1. George Orwell, *The Lion and the Unicorn* (Penguin, 1982), p.118.
2. W. Eichrodt, *Theology of the Old Testament* (SCM Press, 1961), Vol.I, p.250.
3. H. Frankfort, *Ancient Egyptian Religion* (Harper and Row, 1961), p.54.
4. H. Frankfort, *Before Philosophy: The Intellectual Adventure of Ancient Man* (Pelican, 1949), p.120.
5. Exodus 20.2.
6. Exodus 22.23ff.
7. I Samuel 8.11.
8. G.E. Wright and R. Fuller, *The Book of the Acts of God* (Pelican, 1965), p.156.
9. J.A. Soggin, *Introduction to the Old Testament* (SCM Press, 1980).
10. W. Eichrodt, *Theology of the Old Testament* (SCM Press), Vol.I, p.340.
11. Amos 2.7
12. Amos 4.1; 5.7-12; 9.8
13. Amos 5.21-24.
14. Hosea 12.6 It is often said that social problems do not figure in Hosea but cf. 4.1;5.10;10.12.

15. Hosea 10.3.
16. Hosea 1.2.
17. E.g. Amos 5.1; Isaiah 20.2; Jeremiah 19.10, 27.2; Ezekiel 4.5.
18. Isaiah 1.23.
19. Isaiah 1.15-17.
20. Deuteronomy 6.4.
21. Exodus 24.3-8.
22. E.g. Deuteronomy 14.28-15.18;24.10-22 etc.
23. Deuteronomy 23.15.
24. Code of Hammurabi, para.16.
25. E.g. Deuteronomy 22.4;22.10;25.4.
26. E.g. Jeremiah 21.12.
27. E.g. Jeremiah 2.1;3.1;31.20.
28. E.g. Jeremiah 31.31.
29. Isaiah 43.18.
30. Ezekiel 36.26.
31. Leviticus 19.18.
32. Sifra on Leviticus 19.18; Jer. Nedarim 41.3; Bereshit Rabba 24.8.
33. Proverbs 3.11.
34. Proverbs 9.8.

2. AGAPE AND KOINONIA

1. The First Epistle of St Paul to the Corinthians, 13.1.
2. G. Vermes, *Jesus the Jew* (Fontana, 1976), p.130.
3. Isaiah 11.4.
4. Most scholars take the view that while Jesus did have a 'Messianic consciousness' his notion of the Messiah was so different from the popular one that he evaded the issue. In any case the Church adopted the title from the outset partly, no doubt, because this was the charge for which Jesus had been executed but partly also because many expected a speedy second coming which would remove the Roman occupation. Cf. Vermes, pp.140-156.
5. Vermes, p.195 ff., p.216 ff.
6. Isaiah 42.1;56,6-8.
7. Isaiah 42.3.
8. Isaiah 53.3.
9. Isaiah 1-17.

10. Isaiah 53.11.
11. Luke 4.17; Isaiah 61.1.
12. Mark 14.24.
13. Luke 22.24.
14. Matthew 23.2.
15. Acts 2.44; cf. 4.32.
16. V.W. Turner, *The Ritual Process* (Penguin, 1974).
17. A. Van Gennep, *The Rites of Passage* (Routledge and Kegan Paul, 1960).
18. Turner, *ibid.*, p.82.
19. *Ibid.*, p.120.
20. *Ibid.*, pp.126-128.
21. Acts 6.1-6.
22. II Corinthians 3.3.
23. Romans 7.6.
24. II Corinthians 3.6.
25. Romans 13.7.
26. 1 John 4.7.
27. H. Chadwick, *The Early Church* (Penguin, 1967), p.56.
28. A. Kee, *Constantine versus Christ* (SCM Press, 1981).
29. Chadwick, *ibid.*, p.128.
30. *Observer Magazine*, 25 July 1982, p.16.
31. G. Outka, *Agape: an Ethical Analysis* (Yale University Press, 1972).
32. Karl Barth, *Church Dogmatics*, IV/2 (T. & T. Clark, 1958), p.745.
33. W. Shakespeare, Sonnets, 116.
34. Outka *op. cit.*, p.12.
35. *Ibid.*, p.21.
36. S. Kierkegaard, *Works of Love* (Harper, 1962), p.39.
37. A. Nygren, *Agape and Eros* (SPCK, 1957).
38. J. Fletcher, *Situation Ethics* (Westminster Press, 1966), p.87.
39. Outka, *op. cit.*, p.77.
40. *Ibid.*, p.20.
41. *Ibid.*, p.91.
42. Cf. Acts 2.44.
43. Outka, *op. cit.*, p.91.

44. *Ibid.*, p.310.

45. G. Vlastos, 'Justice and Equality' in *Social Justice*, ed. R.B. Brandt (Prentice Hall, 1962), p.88.

3. CHARITY AND EQUITY

1. G. Williams, *Learning the Law* (Stevens and Sons, 1978), p.22.

2. According to Professor S.F.C. Milsom (*Historical Foundations of the Common Law*, Butterworth, 1969, p.169) in early English law the term *usus* 'appears generally to be nothing to do with using but to be a translation of *oeps*'. *Al oeps* was Norman French for 'on the behalf of' so that property held by one person 'to the use' of another would mean 'on behalf of' rather than 'for the use of'. Most early uses were both 'on behalf of' *and* 'for the use of', however, and it may be that the two notions were easily confused. More importantly, this etymological derivation does little to explain where the first settlors of uses found the *model* for their new practice and the Franciscan explanation does at least offer a half-way house between Roman and English conceptions of the 'use'.

3. Henry VIII's *Statute of Uses – 1536* had sought to restore feudal revenue by eradicating uses altogether. But the courts held that the statute did not apply to active uses or grants to corporations to the use of another party.

4. W.K. Jordan, *Philanthropy in Britain 1480-1660* (Allen and Unwin, 1959).

5. G. Jones, *History of the Law of Charity 1532-1827* (Cambridge University Press, 1969), p.19.

6. *Ibid.*, p.31ff.

7. D.H. McMullen, S.G. Maurice and D.B. Parker, *Tudor on Charities* (Sweet and Maxwell, 1967), pp.74-83.

8. The exception to this is, of course, the *Recreational Charities Act 1958*.

9. T.H. White, *The Age of Scandal* (Penguin, 1962), p.166.

10. Jones, *op. cit.*, p.105f.

11. *Ibid.*, p.111.

12. *Ibid.*, p.130.

13. M. Morris, *Voluntary Organisations and Social Progress* (Gollancz, 1955), p.19.

14. *Thetford School Case* (1610) 8 Co. Rep. 131a.

15. *Nathan Report: Report of the Committee on Law and Practice relating to Charitable Trusts.* Cmd. 8710 (HMSO, 1952), p.19.
16. *Ibid.*

4. THE LEGAL MEANING OF CHARITY

1. R.E. Ball, 'Memorandum submitted by the Chief Chancery Master' in *Tenth Report from the Expenditure Committee: Charity Commissioners and their Accountability* (HMSO, 1975), Vol.II, p.174.
2. *Charities Act 1960*, sec.45.
3. *Ibid.*, sec.46.
4. G Jones, *History of the Law of Charity 1532-1827* (Cambridge University Press, 1969), p.121.
5. *Jones v. Williams* (1767), Ambl. 651-2.
6. G. Jones, *op. cit.*, p.122.
7. *Morice v. Bishop of Durham* (1804), 9 Ves. 399; (1805) 10 Ves. 522.
8. *Ibid.* (1805), 10 Ves. 522, 523 *per* Richards *arguendo*.
9. *Ibid.* (1804), 9 Ves. 399, 405 *per* Sir William Grant, M.R.
10. *Scottish Burial Reform and Cremation Society Ltd v. Glasgow Corpn* [1968], A.C. 138, 154.
11. *Morice v. Bishop of Durham* (1805), 10 Ves. 522, 532.
12. *Income Tax Special Purposes Courts v. Pemsel* [1891], A.C. 531, 583.
13. *Re Pinion* [1965], Ch. 85, 107. A more contentious example is the courts' refusal to allow charitable status to a community of cloistered and contemplative nuns because the benefit to mankind of their prayers and the example of pious lives was held too vague and incapable of proof (*Gilmour v. Coats* [1949], A.C. 426).
14. *Verge v. Somerville* [1924], A.C. 496, 499 *per* Lord Wenbury.
15. *Re Smith's Will Trusts* [1962], 1 W.L.R. 763, C.A.
16. *Incorporated Council of Law Reporting for England and Wales v. A.-G.* [1972], Ch. 73, 94.
17. *Bowman v. Secular Society* [1917], A.C. 406.
18. G. Williams, *Learning the Law* (Stevens and Sons, 1978), p.88.
19. There are a number of other, fairly technical legal privileges; a good account is M. Chesterman, *Charities, Trusts and Social Welfare* (Weidenfeld and Nicolson, 1979), pp.206-229.

5. WHO SHALL BENEFIT?

1. *Re Macduff* [1896], 2 Ch. 451, 471 (C.A.).

2. W. Shakespeare, *Troilus and Cressida*, III, ii, 171.

3. *National Anti-Vivisection Society v. I.R.C.* [1948], A.C. 31, 65, *per* Lord Simonds.

4. *Shorter Oxford English Dictionary* (OUP, 1956), v.II, p.1613.

5. *Ibid.*, p.1614.

6. M. Chesterman, *Charities, Trusts and Social Welfare* (Weidenfeld and Nicolson, 1979), p.26.

7. G. Duke, *The Law of Charitable Uses* (1676; ed. R.V. Bridgeman, 1805), p.125 (an abridged version of Moore's *Reading*). Italics added.

8. *Ibid.*, pp.125, 128-30.

9. G. Jones, *History of the Law of Charity 1532-1827* (Cambridge University Press, 1969), p.30 quoting from Moore's original manuscript.

10. *Ibid.*, p.30.

11. *Jones v. Williams* (1767), Amb. 651 *per* Lord Camden.

12. *Att.-Gen. v. Hewer* (1700), 2 Vern. 387.

13. *Att.-Gen. v. Lord Lonsdale* (1827), 1 Sim. 105, 109.

14. Chesterman, *op. cit.*, pp.58-9.

15. *Income Tax Special Purposes Comrs. v. Pemsel* [1891], A.C. 531.

16. *Ibid.* at 591.

17. *Re Lucas* [1922], 2 Ch. 52 at 57, 58 *per* Russell, J.

18. *Re Glyn's Will Trusts* [1950], 2 All E.R. 1150.

19. *Att.-Gen. v. Duke of Northumberland* [1877], 7 Ch.D 745, 752 *per* Sir George Jessel, M.R.

20. *Re White's Will Trusts* [1951], 1 All E.R. 528, 530 *per* Harman, J.

21. *Gilmour v. Coats* [1949], A.C. 426, 449 (H.L.).

22. *National Anti-Vivisection Society v. I.R.C.* [1948], A.C. 31, 65 *per* Lord Simonds.

23. D.H. McMullen et al, *Tudor on Charities* (Sweet and Maxwell, 1967), p.73

24. *I.R.Comrs. v. Baddeley* [1955], A.C. 572, 592.

25. *Re Macduff* [1896], 2 Ch. 451, 471 *per* Lindley, L.J.

26. Sir Thomas Browne, 'Religio Medici' in *The Major Works* ed. C.A. Patrides (Penguin, 1977), p.137.

27. *Williams Trustees v. I.R.C.* [1948], A.C. 447, 457 *per* Lord Simonds.

28. Quoted in B. Gardner, *The Public Schools* (Hamish Hamilton, 1973), p.27.

29. Chesterman, *op. cit.*, p.77.

30. J. Gathorne-Hardy, *The Public School Phenomenon* (Hodder and Stoughton, 1977), p.96. And generally a most entertaining and balanced account of the public schools.

31. *Ibid.*, p.98.

32. A.H. Halsey et. al. *Origins and Destinations: Family, Class and Education in Modern Britain* (Oxford University Press, 1980).

33. *Public Schools Commission. First Report* (HMSO, 1968), v.2 p.297. See also H. Glennerster and G. Wilson, *Paying for Private Schools* (Allen Lane, 1970), *passim*.

34. *Ibid.*, p.296.

35. *Ibid.*, Vol I, p.159.

36. Association of Independent Hospitals and Kindred Organisations, *Yearbook 1982* (ALHKO, 1982).

37. *I.R.Comrs. v. Educational Grants Association* [1967], Ch. 993.

38. *Oppenheim v. Tobacco Securities Trust Co. Ltd.* [1951], A.C. 297.

39. See note 15, *supra*.

40. Ditto, at 583.

41. See note 13, *supra*.

42. *The Abbey, Malvern Wells, Ltd. v. Ministry of Local Government and Planning* [1951], Ch. 728.

43. *Ibid.* at 737.

44. See note 27.

45. *Governors of Campbell College Belfast v. Commissioners of Valuation for Northern Ireland* [1964], 2 All E.R. 705.

46. *Ibid.* at 711 *per* Viscount Radcliffe.

47. See *Tudor on Charity*, pp.9-15.

48. *Milianges v. George Frank (Textiles) Ltd.* [1976], A.C. 443, 469.

49. *Re Resch's Will Trusts* [1969], 1 A.C. 514 (Privy Council).

50. See note 38, *supra*.

51. Ditto at 306, *per* Lord Simonds.

52. T.G. Watkin, 'Charity: the Purport of "Purpose"', in *The Conveyancer and Property Lawyer*, 1978, pp.277-290 provides a useful discussion of this issue.

53. M. Young, 'Hackney survey: support for alternatives', *Where?*, *150*, 218-220.

6. BUILDING A NEW SOCIETY

1. *Sunday Telegraph*, 24 June 1979.

2. W. Shakespeare, *The Merchant of Venice*, Act IV, scene 1, 218.

3. F.J. Gladstone, *Voluntary Action in a Changing World* (Bedford Square Press, 1979) examines the arguments for and against government support for voluntary action. R. Hadley and S. Hatch, *Social Welfare and the State* (Allen and Unwin, 1981), covering similar territory, comes to rather different conclusions.

4. Memorandum by R.E. Ball, in House of Commons Expenditure Committee, *Tenth Report: Charity Commissioners and their Accountability* (HMSO, 1968), v.II, p.178.

5. R. Holman, 'The place of voluntary societies', *Community Care*, 12 November, 1981, pp.16-18.

6. K. Worpole, 'Volunteers for socialism', *New Society*, 29 January 1981, pp.199-200. The changing character of voluntary action is also considered in Gladstone, *op. cit.*, chapter 6, pp.63-75.

7. *Re Cole* [1958], Ch. 877.

8. E.g. by Dankwerts, J. in *Re Sahal's Will Trusts* [1958], 1 W.L.R. 1243.

9. *Re Cole* [1958], Ch. 877 at 888 *per* Lord Romer.

10. *Re Mariette* [1915], 2 Ch. 284.

11. *Re Geere's Will Trusts (No.2)* [1954], C.L.Y.338. The gift was applied *cy-près* because the school already had a swimming pool.

12. M. Chesterman, *Charities, Trusts and Social Welfare* (Weidenfeld & Nicholson, 1979), p.335.

13. As in *Re Sahal's Will Trusts* [1958], 1 W.L.R.1243.

14. *D'Augiar v. Guyana I.R. Comrs.* (1970), 49 A.T.C.33.

15. Throughout 1981 Gallup surveys found that seven out of ten voters saw unemployment as the most urgent problem. See N. Webb and R. Wybrow, *The Gallup Report* (Sphere, 1982), p.68.

16. Letter to War on Want, 7 May 1981.

17. Charity Commission letter of 12 January 1977.

18. Quoted in G. Jones, *History of the Law of Charity 1532-1827* (Cambridge University Press, 1969), p.28.

19. *Ibid.*

20. Letter to War on Want, 10 August 1981.

21. Letter to Northamptonshire RCC, 5 May 1982.

22. *Report of the Charity Commissioners for England and Wales, for the year 1969* (HMSO, 1970), p.10.

23. *Idem.* for 1980, (HMSO, 1981), p.27.

24. *Ibid.*, p.23.

25. *Ibid.*, pp.24-5.

26. *Ibid.*, p.7.

27. *Ibid.*, p.8.

28. M. Chesterman, *Charities, Trusts and Social Welfare* (Weidenfeld and Nicholson, 1979), p.347.

29. *Ibid.*, p.348.

30. A. Steen, giving evidence to the House of Commons Expenditure Committee, *Tenth Report: Charity Commissioners and their Accountability* (HMSO, 1975), v.II, pp.307-12.

31. *Report of the Charity Commissioners, 1978* (HMSO, 1979), p.28.

32. *Lord Nuffield v. I.R. Comrs.* (1946), 175 L.T. 465.

33. Charity Commission letter 26 February 1981.

34. Charity Commission letter 5 February 1982.

35. *Voluntary Organisations: An NCVO Directory, 1982/3* (Bedford Square Press, 1982), p.92.

36. *Ibid.*, p.69.

37. Wolfenden Committee, *The Future of Voluntary Organisations* (Croom Helm, 1977), *passim.*

38. Personal communication.

39. *Hansard,* 22 April 1982, col.677.

40. As reported in *Report of the Charity Commissioners 1980* (HMSO, 1981), p.21. The case was *I.R. Comrs v. McMullen and others* [1980], 2 W.L.R.416; 1 All E.R. 884.

41. Charity Commission letter 19 June 1981.

42. Goodman Commission, *Charity Law and Voluntary Organisations* (Bedford Square Press, 1976), p.23.

43. *Camille and Henry Dreyfus Foundation Inc. v. I.R. Comrs* [1954], Ch. 672.

44. The author speaks from recent personal experience. A trust to preserve historic monuments in Egypt was finally accepted as charitable but only after some argument.

45. Goodman Committee, *op. cit.*, p.39.

46. *Ibid.*, p.122.

7. CHARITY AND POLITICS

1. Benjamin Franklin, *Maxims . . . Prefixed to Poor Richard's Almanac* (1758).

2. *Report of the Charity Commissioners for England and Wales for the Year 1981* (HMSO, 1982), p.21.

3. *Bowman v. Secular Society* [1917], A.C. 406, 442.

4. H. Chadwick, *The Early Church* (Penguin, 1967), p.60.

5. *Bowman v. Secular Society* [1917], A.C. 406, 442.

6. *De Themmines v. de Bonneval* (1828), 5 Russ. 288, 7 L.J.O.S. Ch. 35.

7. *National Anti-Vivisection Society v. I.R.Comrs.* [1947], 2 All E.R. 217.

8. *Re Hopkinson* [1949], 1 All E.R. 346.

9. *Re Strakosch* [1949], Ch. 529 (CA).

10. *Anglo-Swedish Society v. I.R.Comrs.* [1931], 47 T.L.R. 295.

11. *Re Buxton* [1962], 41 T.C. 235.

12. *McGovern v. A.-G.* [1981], 3 All E.R. 493, 506.

13. E.g. H. Picarda, *The Law and Practice Relating to Charities* (Butterworth, 1977), p.117.

14. *McGovern v. A.-G.* [1981], 3 All E.R. 493, 506 *per* Slade, J.

15. Goodman Committee, *Charity Law and Voluntary Organisations* (Bedford Square Press, 1976), p.149.

16. D. Wilson, 'Does generosity have to come but once a year?', *The Times,* 14 December 1981.

17. Nathan Committee, *Report of the Committee on the Law and Practice relating to Charitable Trusts.* Cmd 8710 (HMSO, 1952), p.13.

18. *Re Strakosch* [1949], Ch. 529.

19. *Re Buxton* [1962], 41 T.C. 235.

20. *Re Harwood* [1936], Ch. 285.

21. *The American Restatement,* Trusts 2d, s.374, comment 1.

22. *Parkhurst v. Burrill* (1917), 117 N.E. 39.

23. *McGovern v. A.-G.* [1981], 3 All E.R. 493.

24. *Jackson v. Phillips* (1867), 96 Mass. 539.

25. *McGovern v. A.-G.* [1981], 3 All E.R. 493, 508.

26. B.W. Walker, 'Charities and politics', *The Friend,* November 1979.

27. B. Wren, *The Politics of Charity* (Wren, 1978), p.3.

28. Quoted in J. Madely, 'When the relief of poverty leads charities to seek political change', *The Diplomatist,* December 1981.

29. J. Rossiter, 'Taking sides: the Church in Central America', *Voluntary Action,* Summer 1982.

30. *The Times,* 20 September 1980.

31. *Evening Standard,* 16 August 1982.

32. Charity Commission letter, 12 February 1975, quoted in: V. Houghton, 'The Changing Role of Charities', in *Perimeters of Social Repair, Proceedings of the Fourteenth Symposium of the Eugenics Society* (London, 1978), p.20.

33. *National Anti-Vivisection Society v. I.R.Comrs.* [1947], 2 All E.R. 217.

34. *Re,Hopkinson* [1949], 1 All E.R. 346,350 *per* Vaisey, J; *Re Bushnell* [1975], 1 All E.R. 721 *per* Goulding, J.

35. *Re Hopkinson* [1949], 1 All E.R. 346, 352.

36. *National Anti-Vivisection Society v. I.R.Comrs.* [1947], A.C. 31, 61, *per* Lord Simonds.

37. *Ibid.* at 76 *per* Lord Normand.

8. RUSTY CURBS?

1. W. Shakespeare, *Henry IV,* Pt I, I, ii.

2. Memorandum to the House of Commons Expenditure Committee, *Tenth Report: Charity Commissioners and their Accountability* (HMSO, 1975), v.II, p.18.

3. See chapter 3.

4. Information supplied by the Charity Commission.

5. Memorandum from B.H. Woods to the House of Commons Expenditure Committee, *op. cit.,*p.283.

6. *Ibid.,* Inland Revenue oral evidence, p.92.

7. *Halsbury's Laws of England* (4th ed.) v.V, para 696).

8. House of Commons Expenditure Committee, *op. cit.,* p.121-2.

9. R.D. Woodall, 'Do the Charity Commissioners always consider local needs?', *District Councils Review,* November 1981, p.263.

10. Memorandum from J.D. Livingstone-Booth to the House of Commons Expenditure Committee, *op. cit.,* v.II, p.288.

11. *Registration of Charities in Scotland: Report of a Working Party* (Scottish Council for Social Service, 1972).

12. The Newark Committee: *Charity Committee Report*, Cmd.396 (Belfast HMSO, 1956), p.10.

13. Memorandum from the Charity Commissioners to the House of Commons Expenditure Committee, *op. cit.*, p.19.

14. *Ibid.*, p.351.

15. B. Whitaker, *The Foundations* (Penguin, 1979) provides a lively account.

16. *Gulbenkian 1982: Policies and Activities 1982; Projects Initiated 1981* (Gulbenkian Foundation, 1982), p.5.

17. Personal communication.

9. TIME FOR A NEW START?

1. Johnathan Swift, *A Tritical Essay upon the Faculties of the Mind.*

2. Charity Law Reform Committee, *Charity Law – only a new start will do* (CLRC, 1974).

3. *Ibid.*, p.4.

4. *Ibid.*, p.5.

5. *Ibid.*

6. *Tenth Report from the Expenditure Committee: Charity Commissioners and their Accountability* (HMSO, 1975), v.II, p.100. Oral evidence given by Mr. A.J. Gower Isaac, Under Secretary, Board of Inland Revenue.

7. *Ibid.*, p.250.

8. *The Radcliffe Report: Final Report of the Royal Commission on the Taxation of Profits and Income*, Cmd. 9474 (HMSO, 1955), p.55.

9. S. Surrey, *Pathways to Tax Reform: The Concept of Tax Expenditures* (Harvard University Press, 1973).

10. I. Kristol, 'Taxes, poverty, and equality', *Public Interest, 37* (Fall, 1974), pp.14-15.

11. *Radcliffe Report*, p.56.

12. Goodman Committee, *Charity Law and Voluntary Organisations* (Bedford Square Press, 1976), p.145.

13. *Ibid.*

14. *Ibid.*

15. See chapters 3 and 4.

16. E.g. Professor Adrian Webb, 'Voluntary social action: in search of a policy?', *Journal of Voluntary Action Research, 8* (Jan 1979), pp.8-16, at p.12.

17. Chapter 5 discussed the Labour Party's reluctance to tackle private hospitals.

18. Expenditure Committee of the House of Lords, *Tenth Report: Charity Commissioners and their Accountability* (HMSO, 1975), v.I, p.xxxiv.

19. *Ibid.*, p.xxxii.

20. L.A. Sheridan, 'Waiting for Goodman', *Anglo-American Law Review* (1976) 5, pp.153-172 at p.154.

21. Expenditure Committee, *ibid.*, p.xvi.

22. *Ibid.*, p.xii.

23. This paragraph is loosely based on (a) Lord Simonds' distinction in *I.R.Comrs. v. Baddeley* [1955], A.C. 572, 592 and (b) the proposals contained in the *First Report of the Public Schools Commission* (HMSO, 1968), p.161, para. 366.

24. Rt. Hon. Sir Geoffrey Howe, Chancellor of the Exchequer, *Lecture to the Conservative Political Centre Summer School in Cambridge* (Conservative Central Office, 1982), p.22

25. *Hansard,* 16 December 1981, cols. 404-5.

10. PIECEMEAL REFORM

1. Edmund Burke: (a) Speech on Conciliation with America, 1775; (b) Speech at Bristol previous to the Election, 1780.

2. John Milton, *Areopagitica,* 1644.

3. Goodman Committee, *Charity Law and Voluntary Organisations* (Bedford Square Press, 1976) pp.123-5.

4. *Ibid.*, p.47.

5. *Ibid.*, p.46.

6. *Report of the Charity Commissioners for England and Wales for the year 1969* (HMSO, 1970), p.10.

7. Expenditure Committee of the House of Commons, *Tenth Report: Charity Commissioners and their Accountability,* (HMSO, 1975), v.I, p.xiv.

8. Goodman Committee, *op. cit.*, p.44.

9. *Ibid.*, pp.45-7.

10. See chapter 7.

11. Treasury regulation 501 (c) (3).

12. John Milton, *op. cit.*

13. B. Cox, *Civil Liberties in Britain* (Penguin, 1975).

14. Hansard, 15 June 1982, col.734.

15. It was recommended by the Goodman Committee, the House of Commons Expenditure Committee and the Charity Law Reform Committee.

16. As note 15.

17. The Royal Commission on Legal Services, *Final Report*, Cmnd.7648 (HMSO, 1979), v.I, p.51.

18. But cf. *Ibid.*, pp.128-130.

19. *Ibid.*, p.180.

20. Memorandum by J.D. Livingstone-Booth, in Expenditure Committee of the House of Commons, *Tenth Report: Charity Commissioners and their Accountability* (HMSO, 1975), v.II, p.286.

21. *Ibid.*, p.289.

22. *Charities Act, 1960*, 1(3), italics added.

CONCLUSION: THE SPIRIT OF CHARITY

1. The 'Beveridge Report': *Social Insurance and Allied Services*, Cmnd.6404 (HMSO, 1942).

2. Miguel de Cervantes, *The Adventures of Don Quixote*, transl. J.M. Cohen (Penguin, 1950), pp.68-87.

3. L. Tolstoy, *What Then Must We Do?* transl. Maude (Oxford University Press, 1935).

4. B. Wren, 'Looking for the elephant', *One World, 12*, (World Council of Churches, Geneva, Dec. 1975), pp. 20-21.

5. William Blake: 'The Clod and the Pebble'.

Index

INDEX

P. 32. PRAISE